ABOUT THE PEOPLE?

by Terry Sanford

Harper & Row, Publishers

This book about politics and education is lovingly dedicated to my mother, Betsy Martin Sanford, who heightened my interest in education, and to my father, Cecil L. Sanford, who heightened my interest in politics

Acknowledgments

Unhappily, it is not possible to acknowledge the efforts nor mention the individual work of the loyal participants who built the story of state government told in this book. But the thousands of Bill Whites, Clarks, Younts and Faircloths, the Statons, Bensons, Newtons and Joyners, the Henleys, Highs, McLeans and Teagues, although unmentioned, must surely know I understand where the credit belongs.

For reading the manuscript and making worthwhile suggestions and essential corrections, I thank Eli Evans, Gibson Prather, Hugh Cannon, Joel Fleishman, Richard Walser, Epps Ready, Raymond Stone, Andy Jones, David Ethridge, Jay Jenkins, and Graham Jones. I am most grateful to Mrs. Patton Wheeler who protected my consistency by her careful research.

TERRY SANFORD

Fayetteville
North Carolina

Contents

Foreword
by James B. Conant

The story of what happened in the field of education in North Carolina from 1961 to 1964 needed to be told. No one could tell the story better than the man who was governor of the state during those four years. For it was his imaginative leadership that made possible the changes which were not only significant for his state but in many instances useful as models in other states as well. The account of these changes and especially the way they were brought about provides a series of fascinating case histories in practical state politics. A study of these cases throws much light on the wide range of problems that face those who today are concerned with improving the instructional facilities available to all the people.

In recent years there have been a number of books by laymen highly critical of those in charge of our public schools. And now the wave of criticism seems to be engulfing our colleges and universities. What is all too often lacking in these appraisals of the American scene is an accurate portrayal of the tasks which society now demands that educators undertake. Any connection between public finance and public education is usually passed by in silence. Here is a book by a governor who at the outset of his career as a public servant squarely faced the fact that better public schools cost money. He campaigned on the issue; he was elected and then at once persuaded the legislature to make good on his promises, even though this involved a substantial increase in state taxes.

Those readers who have some knowledge of the archaic and chaotic way we raise money for our public schools will recognize that North Carolina is almost unique among the states. In this state a very large proportion of the costs of elementary and secondary education is paid from state funds. To my mind the pattern might well be copied by those states in which the public schools are largely financed by local real estate taxes, with the result that there are gross irregularities in the quality of education among the different school districts. It in no way diminishes one's admiration for what Governor Sanford accomplished to note that the financial structure of education in his state gives to the legislature and to the governor, as the political leader, crucial roles in improving education. The chapters of this book, I hope, forecast not only the kind of leadership we may expect to develop at the state level but also the kind of organization that enables a farseeing statesman to be effective.

Governor Sanford, through his actions, has already put all who believe in public education in his debt. His recounting of these actions in the pages that follow adds to our indebtedness. As an author he captures the interest of the reader by apt anecdotes and then proceeds with a quotable sentence to make a telling point. The fact that what he writes is based on his own experience makes his analysis of present-day issues something more than a theoretical discussion. In short, this is a unique book by an unusual person whose views are as stimulating as his leadership in North Carolina was effective.

Preface

This is the story of an American state not content with the quality and extent of the education available to its children. It is the story of a state dedicated to the proposition that its hopes for human progress depend on educated people. It is an account of North Carolina's efforts from the beginning of 1961 through 1964, the term of one administration, to commit itself to education as the vital tool for the creation of new jobs, for the development of a more substantial and diversified economic structure, for the elimination of the causes of poverty, the easing of prejudices and racial discrimination, the fulfillment of individual aspirations, and the cultivation of all human capacities.

The southwest corner of North Carolina converges with Georgia and Tennessee near two Tennessee towns, one called Copperhill and the other Ducktown. At this place there lies a vast and shameful scar on the earth covering miles of once green and beautiful mountain country. The interested visitor may read in his tour book that defoliation and the resulting erosion have made the entire area "similar to the Badlands of the West." Unlike the

West, however, this scar is not the result of nature. Early in this century an untold number of trees was felled to feed the fires under huge piles of smoldering copper ore, sending forth noxious fumes to lay bare whatever vegetation remained. Today the majestic mountains, with their naked clay and rocks exposed in ugliness and uselessness, look out to the traveler as a stark indictment of man's neglect.

Belatedly, there are enlightened programs under way to reclaim the land and rebuild the forests. In one place after another, all across the nation, we have come to realize that we cannot afford to waste our soil and rivers and woodlands. But what about our human resources? What about the people? What about the countless thousands whose lives are so dulled by poverty that the American dream is incomprehensible to them? What about those whose education is so limited that they cannot profit from our rich cultural history and share in our literary and artistic heritage? What about the people who are not trained to take part in our rapidly changing economic life, and are thus condemned to exist on the outer edges of American prosperity? What about those whose ignorance and inadequate education diminish the contribution they might have made to society? Is all this waste not a painful scar upon the earth, a mighty indictment of man's neglect?

I believe that government is charged with the duty of providing the means for the fulfillment of the human spirit and the fruitful use of all talents. By starting with sound, meaningful education, we make it possible for each person to add his own gift to his generation, to become a part of the progress of man. In turn, the individual makes the nation stronger, defends against its enemies, adds to its wealth, and carries forward its ideals and faith.

To tell this North Carolina story I have attempted to document the reasons for our failure to reach so many of our young people, the method of setting goals, the strategy for gaining public support, and the measures of improvement or innovation attempted or achieved.

Essentially this is the account of how political leaders and educational leaders joined in a working partnership, each trusting the other, both intent on using education as the instrument for creative development of human resources.

The book deals with education and is not intended to be a report of all the activities of state government. I have omitted such indispensable public functions as roads, mental hospitals, conservation, prison rehabilitation, water resources, and industrial development. Obviously all these responsibilities of government, and many others, including the protection of civil rights, are influenced by the emphasis placed on education.

It has not been possible to list every step of every program, although sufficient statistical and technical information has been included, I hope, to assure a solid factual background. For example, a few paragraphs describe our Curriculum Study which was designed to improve the courses in our schools. The reports and guides resulting from that study comprise thousands of pages and are available to those who need such information in detail. Many other programs are mentioned, any one of which would require as many pages as this entire volume for a full discussion. There is no attempt to be technical, for I have never pretended to be an educator, nor have I considered myself any kind of expert in educational affairs. I have written as a public official, convinced that the citizens of a state will rise to support improvement of the educational system if provided a rallying point, and convinced that educators will rise to greater productivity if given the challenge and the support.

Neither does the story intend to suggest that North Carolina knows all the answers, nor even to claim that it has found all the questions. It is the beginning of an answer one state has attempted to give to the question asked of itself, "But what about the people?"

Woven inevitably through this entire story is the thesis that state government must accept and assert broader responsibilities for education, thereby becoming more effective in the service of its people and more viable in the advancement of its democratic purposes.

. . . "Yes but the people what about the people?"
Sometimes as though the people is a child to be
pleased or fed
Or again a hoodlum you have to be tough with
And seldom as though the people is a caldron and
a reservoir
Of the human reserves that shape history . . .
                    —Carl Sandburg, *The People, Yes*
                    Sec. 86

CHAPTER I : Inventory of Weakness

THE DECEMBER WIND was biting through my wool sweater, and I was wishing that I had never left home to look for a Christmas tree. My older brother, ten years of age and bigger than I, was carrying the ax slanted across his shoulder like a soldier's rifle. Our father was setting the pace, which was a little too brisk for me. I wanted a warm fire. I wanted to be inside.

Then around the curve in the wooded trail there it was, looming like the Promised Land. An unpainted shanty was all it was and the front door had even fallen off, but there was a thriving column of smoke surging from the chimney. Inside, the flaming glow rivaled the magnificence of the midday summer sun, and it was obvious that the door hadn't fallen off at all. It was being used as firewood.

Presiding over this warming utopia, in an otherwise empty room, was a little man with a red face and a strange odor on his breath. The odor, in later years I was to learn, was canned heat, which in those days of prohibition was about as handy a source of drinking alcohol as you were likely to find.

He welcomed us in and we crouched around the fireplace until the door was all consumed. It wasn't very long. When the fire burned out he went his way, his World War I overcoat almost dragging the ground.

My daddy knew him. He called him Johnny and they exchanged some small talk about how cold it was, and how good the fire felt, and how it was only a short time until Christmas. I wanted to ask him what he was doing, and where he was going, and who was he anyhow. But I didn't. I waited and asked my daddy, after he had gone.

What was Johnny up to? My daddy said, "No good, I'm afraid." What did he do? "Nothing, most of the time." Where did he live? "Wherever he can beat somebody out of the rent."

His name was Johnny Randolph. I knew his boys at school. One of them, Honey, was about my age, ragged, dirty, a troublemaker by the teachers' standards, profane at the age of six, thief of ten-cent-store items at the age of seven, one of those who came to school most of the time without any lunch bag.

Honey wasn't unique. There were many like him at school. They didn't do well, and ultimately they drifted away, or their families moved maybe, or they just weren't there any more. I hadn't heard of the word "dropouts," but that is what they were.

I remember hearing another story about Honey. He couldn't have been fourteen years old, maybe only twelve. In his way he was already a colorful character. One deputy sheriff was pleased to sit around the courthouse lawn and tell about the time he took Honey to the reformatory. That is how I knew he had been caught breaking into a store. With great guffawing, the deputy described how Honey entered the admission office. He pushed back the two deputies with both of his scrawny little arms and yelled, to the delight and entertainment of the reformatory staff members, "Clear the damn way! Here comes John Dillinger the Second!"

The next time I heard his name I was sitting in the Governor's chair, talking to a lawyer. He wanted commutation for a young prisoner who had been studying to get a high school diploma in our prison school system. The plea had some merit. The name was totally unfamiliar to me until the lawyer said, "You may remember his father, Honey Randolph. He was killed by a train several years ago down in South Carolina."

Into my mind flashed this cycle of tragedy and failure. The burning door, the army coat, the canned heat odor, the school dropout, the pathetic braggadocio at the reformatory, the manslaughter conviction of the third generation.

Somehow this boy, born into a house of despair, with incomplete education and no skill, killing a friend in a drunken brawl, was an instantaneous revelation of both the erosion and the repair of the human spirit.

The helping, encouraging, sympathetic hand extended by an enlightened prison system had been grasped by the third generation of ignorance and poverty. True, he hadn't proved himself, but the spirit, while badly mangled, was still alive. We could take him by the hand; we could lead him to self-respect and productivity. Or could we?

If we could not, then it was certain that yet another generation of ignorance and poverty would be visited upon us. If we could redeem this boy, his children could move to brighter opportunities.

Could we break this cycle of poverty? Could we break it for the Randolph boy, and for tens of thousands like him, both in and out of prison, both on and off relief rolls, both black and white, all born into poverty which breeds ignorance and ignorance which breeds poverty?

This young prisoner and his father and his grandfather were pitiful examples of the erosion of human resources from generation to generation. This was proof of neglect. This was our failure to protect the greatest of America's assets, her people, all of them.

In Honey Randolph's boy, the tragedy was sharply in focus. But what about the others? What about the high school valedictorian who started in the first grade with Honey? He is now very respectable and not at all in prison, but his abilities have not been fully used because funds for a college education were not available. This is equally tragic waste of America's human resources. And what about all the boys and girls between these two extremes—those who drop out of school, those who never learn to read, those who can but do not learn a skill, those with superior academic or artistic talents never uncovered? Like silt in a great river washing out to form a useless marshland, this potential for the development of North Carolina, and America, has been swept away in wasted lives.

Education develops human resources. Human resources, in turn, make a nation whatever it is to be. It seemed to me, when I pondered running for governor of North Carolina, that education must of necessity be our primary concern. In the first place, we were behind in the comparative ratings with other states. This meant our children, generally speaking, started life with a competitive disadvantage.

Furthermore, education in the formal sense was not reaching enough people in any state, so even if we provided huge additional sums of money we would not be doing the job of total education. Even in those states and areas where comparative per pupil expenditures were high far too many children were not benefiting very much.

I decided I would make it my business to improve our system of developing human resources. I decided I would run for governor and make education the star by which we would sail.

In many ways the Governor's office can be the most creative political office in the nation. Generally its occupant can remain close to the people, frequently he can cut through the bureaucracy which often hampers a larger governmental operation, and always he can exercise his imagination and exert his considerable political power to improve conditions as he finds them.

It is difficult to come up with a definition of government

which doesn't directly involve people. The Constitution of the United States proclaims that our purpose as "a more perfect Union" is to establish justice (for the people), to insure domestic tranquillity (for the people), to provide for the common defense (of the people), to promote the general welfare (of the people), and to secure the blessings of liberty to ourselves (the people) and our posterity (our people).

Indeed, if government is not for the express purpose of lifting the level of civilization by broadening the opportunities in life for its people, what is its purpose? Even the protective instruments, such as police and military, are to protect the people in their pursuit of the fruits of civilization.

How, then, can a government evaluate the chance of success available to its people? Admittedly the chance varies with different civilizations. A child of India does not have the odds of success stacked into the deck the Scandinavian child has at birth. The child of the United States has much better odds than most for drawing the winning cards, but is there some inexorable law which demands that a fixed percentage must not find success or fulfillment of life?

Surely our compassion is not so sterile that we must continue to fail the Honey Randolphs. Surely our civilization is not so frail that we can consider our duty done at a time when our education is missing upwards of 50 percent of our population.

Government is not something passive, not our kind of government. It has built into it the spirit of outreach, the concern for every individual. Look at the verbs in the Constitution's Preamble—*establish, insure, provide, promote, secure.* All these connote action, and all suggest that we must constantly be striving to improve the opportunities of our people.

That is why, as a candidate and later as a governor, my first question was whether all children born in North Carolina had a fair chance to develop, to compete, to achieve, to use fully all the talents with which God had endowed them. I really didn't need to ask the question because I knew the answer. Too many were failing to achieve, develop, and compete. To do something about it, I first had to pick out our weaknesses. Where were we failing people? How? What might be done to correct these failures?

I suspected that North Carolina was not much different from other states in its failures. My travels about the country and my meetings with other governors have confirmed this suspicion. We were all failing. We all had so much to do.

No individual likes to take stock of his shortcomings, and I am sure a time comes as we grow older when we might as well quit worrying about what we aren't. We might very well conclude that it is too late to improve very much. But it pays a young person to look for his faults while he can correct them. In this respect we are a youthful nation and a youthful state, and we have a long life ahead of us, and we can and must always be seeking improvement. So we must inventory our failures and flaws, even if it hurts. This is the beginning of progress.

North Carolina contains about 52,000 square miles. It is a state of exceptional diversity. In the west the Blue Ridge and Great Smoky Mountains converge to create a wondrous area of colorful beauty, attracting tourists from all over America. Here are found the highest peaks east of the Rockies. Inadequate transportation has retarded industrial development, a deficiency that can be and is being overcome by engineering and construction funds.

The mountains drop down to meet the Piedmont Plateau, which comprises about half of the state, where began most of our industry, a result of the early harnessing of the river resources. Now the major problem is the harnessing of the forces of growth, so that the rapid economic advancement does not bring crowded and unwholesome living environment. And there is a continuing appeal for a greater diversity of industry, bringing extended strength to an economy which already leads the nation in the manufacture of textiles, tobacco, and furniture.

Eastern North Carolina is known as the Coastal Plain and has always been fertile farming country. Mechanization and a shaky tobacco market have lessened the need for farm labor, and determined efforts to attract new industry are providing some fresh opportunities. This country is bordered by a 320-mile coastline including an offshore chain of barrier reefs called the Outer Banks. It was here that in 1587 Sir Walter Raleigh's first settlement was established, later to be named "The Lost Colony."

All this scenic wealth makes the state a "variety vacationland," tempting residents and visitors with fishing in clear mountain streams, sunning on sandy ocean shores, camping, boating, or playing at the "golf capital of the world." These resources have been directed to the betterment of the economy and life of the people. The same diversity also means that the state has rich counties and poor counties, sparsely settled and heavily populated counties, remote counties and counties which enjoy the best of communications and transportation.

During the days of "The Great Depression" many counties found it impossible to continue support of their schools. Some paid teachers in scrip, some went into debt heavily, some simply did not meet the payrolls, and all found their systems of education in jeopardy. It was at this time that the state assumed the responsibility for the operation of the public schools. Governor J. C. B. Ehringhaus, whose political courage I have always admired, insisted on a new tax structure, the state sales tax, the first in the nation.

"If it is a choice between a sales tax on the one hand and a decent school on the other, I stand for the school," he told the General Assembly. The state accepted the primary responsibility for the operating expenses, principally teacher pay, and the counties retained responsibility for building costs and maintenance. The counties were permitted and encouraged to add local taxes to provide additional teachers and to pay teacher supplements. This remains the basic pattern of school support in North Carolina.

The action in the thirties was in keeping with our history. It should be remembered that North Carolina had been heavily laden with many unusual burdens. In common with the rest of the South, the aftermath of the Civil War had brought our state economic repression, discriminatory freight rates, restricted financial credit, and political disorder. North Carolina in 1858, with 155,000 pupils enrolled in some 3,700 common schools, had what the United States Commissioner of Education was later to describe as "beyond dispute, the best system of public instruction in the fourteen Southern states east of the Mississippi previous to the outbreak of the Civil War." After the war it had very little means of building or supporting schools.

Gerald Johnson tells of an uncle who had taken a degree at the University of North Carolina just in time to spend four years in the Confederate Cavalry. He returned from war ruined, like everyone else. His young nephew was visiting one midsummer noon when the uncle, caked with dust, came in to dinner from the cornfield where he had been stripping fodder. The boy pumped water while the former scholar and soldier mopped his face and arms.

Then, in Johnson's words, his uncle "looked at me with a sardonic grin and broke into thundering strophes of one of the Georgics of Vergil: *O fortunatos nimium, sua si bona norint, agricolas*—O most happy farmers, if only they knew their good fortune!

"The small boy was merely startled by the rolling Latin measures, but an aging man knows now that he had there before his eyes the South triumphant." The uncle had been ruined, not by his own fault, and faced a life of hard labor, with small hope of ever attaining a life of ease. "Yet in the stifling heat of the cornfield, in a land of poverty and defeat, so far was he from broken that the ear of his mind could hear a great poet singing, and his stout heart could laugh at the absurdity of human fate."

The same spirit of North Carolina triumphant was exemplified by Charles Brantley Aycock, elected governor in 1900. At a time when the recovery of a number of Southern states was retarded by less statesmanlike leadership, he mounted a remarkable crusade for education.

He told the state at his inauguration: "We enter an era of industrial development. Growth in that direction is dependent upon intelligence—not the intelligence of the few, but of all. . . ."

He went on to say that "On a hundred platforms, to half the voters of the State, in the late campaign, I pledged the State, its strength, its heart, its wealth to universal education. . . . It shall be my constant aim and effort, during the four years that I shall endeavor to serve the people of this State, to redeem this most solemn of all our pledges."

For four magnificent years education came first. Governor Aycock and Superintendent of Schools Charles D. McIver stumped the state to build support for school taxes, higher teacher salaries, longer terms, and better buildings. During his four-year term of office new schoolhouses were built on the average of one a day.

This accomplishment and many other achievements by North Carolina continue to stir the pride of her citizens. But there were many things about North Carolina's educational system that stirred my concern when I prepared to take office at the end of 1960. It was scant consolation that the name of almost any state in the Union might well have fit at the heading of our list of shortcomings. Our job was to get the inadequacies into focus, and then do something about them.

To help me define the needs and the action for school improvement, I leaned on many people. Reid Ross is an educator who would do an outstanding job in any state. He comes from the Scottish communities at the head of the Cape Fear River and serves as superintendent of the schools in my home town. Dr. Charles F. Carroll is the elected State Superintendent of Public

Instruction, first appointed by agreement of two governors to fill a vacancy, and he enjoys the complete confidence of the school professionals. Dallas Herring, a manufacturer, Latin scholar, chairman of the State Board of Education, is without question one of the most imaginative lay leaders of education in America. Charles G. Rose, Jr., a lawyer, and Dr. Guy B. Phillips, retired Dean of the School of Education of the University of North Carolina at Chapel Hill, were members of the State Board of Education. Isaac Epps Ready was a school superintendent who had been brought to Raleigh by Governor Hodges, upon the recommendation of the State Board of Education to head the Curriculum Study. Dick Phillips is dean of the University of North Carolina Law School. My own mother, who has taught school most of the time since 1908, A. C. Dawson, a former superintendent, Raymond Stone, then a graduate student, Wallace Hyde, a former high school basketball coach and teacher, A. B. Gibson and Glenn Robertson, former presidents of the North Carolina Education Association, my wife who is a former school teacher, Sam Edwards and Bert Ishee, school principals—all these had a daily awareness of the needs of the schools.

These are some of the people who in 1960 helped me shape the campaign proposals for education. Furthermore, as a State Senator in 1953 I had been exposed to the policy and budget requests, and as a candidate stressing education as the primary need of the state I attracted much advice from school personnel and patrons. In addition, I made it my business to read carefully the recent studies of American education, especially those conducted by Dr. James Bryant Conant.

Out of this cross section of information and advice I drew my own conclusions about our shortcomings, and made my own inventory of weaknesses:

1. With some few local exceptions, our public schools were not paying adequate salaries, the classrooms were overcrowded, libraries were inadequate, and laboratories were poorly equipped.

2. The courses of study in the high school were slanted too much toward college preparation, and generally the curriculum was behind the times.

3. Too many of our high schools were too small, and the resistance to consolidation was widespread.

4. We were developing a good system of industrial education, but it was not inclusive enough, and it attracted only those who had the time and money to attend, missing many who needed training or retraining the most.

5. By actual count only about 50 percent of the number who started school in the fall of 1947 had been graduated in the spring of 1959.

6. Too many teen-agers, school dropouts, were standing around on the streets, with no training, waiting to get into serious trouble, and destined to contribute nothing to society. Most of them did not comprehend the need for education, and did not understand the procedures for going back to school. We were not recruiting.

7. We had no plan for training workers who were leaving the farm in the face of mechanization and shrinking acreage quotas.

8. The retarded child was generally neglected, with a few schools here and there for the educable and almost none for the trainable. We did have institutions for custodial cases, but even here not enough facilities were available.

9. The talented and exceptionally bright child, in most places, found little to sustain his interest and no additional challenges or specially designed programs.

10. Our colleges were overcrowded, and our university, still one of the leaders in the nation, was in danger of being left behind by progress being made at other universities.

11. Too many bright students, who should have been going to college, were not going because of the costs involved or because of lack of encouragement.

12. Too many worthwhile young people, not "college mate-

rial," were going to college when they should not, and subsequently failing, because we did not provide training opportunities beyond the high school which satisfied both their capabilities and their parents' ambitions.

13. We did not have suitable training programs for prisoners who often got into trouble because of a lack of earning capacity, and who probably could keep out of future trouble if the state provided training in skills.

14. Our welfare, health, and employment services had no working relationship with our school system for the purpose of directing to additional education those who could use appropriate training to obtain jobs or improve their status.

15. We did not understand that many young Negroes were neglecting or abandoning their education because every day they saw too many examples within their own race which illustrated to them that education was not likely to lead to jobs commensurate with their abilities and aspirations.

16. We did not understand that "the children of poverty" could never take advantage of our school system which, because of their environments, was a totally strange world to them. Coming from homes that neither used nor understood the printed word, they started school with almost insurmountable obstacles. We had no program to give them the special encouragement and orientation they required to survive in our established structure of education.

17. We were not doing much planning ahead for education, and were not prepared to seek and take full advantage of new ideas and changing methods. We had no comprehensive program of research and evaluation to support our massive investments in education.

This inventory of weaknesses and failures enabled us to begin to shape a program of educational progress. While taking due note of our past achievements, and due credit for our accomplishments, it was appropriate to remember Heywood Broun's comment, "No body politic is healthy until it begins to itch." We were preparing to make more progress by listing our failures. Behind this listing marched a horde of tragic stories. There was so much to do. Erosion of human resources has become the most demanding challenge of our times. I believed that we should concern ourselves not only with a wasted life but also with those talents only partially used. We were not just seeking better schools, but would look for imaginative and experimental programs which would break through the accepted patterns to reach effectively all children, whatever their talents or limitations.

I was also convinced that even if all states shared these defects, in varying degrees and intensity, the duty to take the initiative belonged to the state. The challenge was too massive for a single federal program, which would have been too late and too cumbersome anyhow. Each state could move in its own way, not refusing or eschewing federal participation, but neither waiting for some total solution to be provided by federal action. I felt that the states were in the best position to stop the waste of human talents, and that North Carolina should exercise the leadership incumbent upon it. I was determined that my four years would be devoted to rebuilding what lay waste, to saving what could be saved, to working for the young, and to charting for the future until we were using all our human resources.

No one seeking to accomplish these purposes would seriously contend that education, no matter how broadly defined, is the whole story. It is, however, a necessary prelude and the beginning of the whole story.

But first we had to win the election.

CHAPTER II : Action

for the Average

To BEGIN a program of action to overcome these many enumerated weaknesses in our system of education was a somewhat awesome task. One weekend when I was sitting with members of my campaign staff and others attempting to define what we hoped to accomplish, a high school principal told us a story about his wife.

"When she started spring house cleaning last spring," he said, "she reminded me of the many things she had to do. She said she looked around and decided she could have started in the living room or in the kitchen. She could have started with the vacuum cleaner or the window washer. Wherever she looked there was a pile of work to be done. She could have started by taking out the rugs or taking in the paintbrush.

"With so much to do, and so many places to start, and so much work all around, she said she just threw up her hands and sat down to rest, weary at the very sight of all the work. She figured she might as well wait until next spring."

He made his point: "It appears to me that we have been sitting down too long because of the magnitude and complexity of school problems. But the time has come to get up and go to work. The way to start is to pick a starting place, any starting place."

We had gathered many ideas and a fair concept of what should be done. And now we found it necessary to outline our intentions for the public in some detail as we developed the campaign.

While I was certain that the improvement of education was my chief reason for running, I am not sure that in the beginning we deliberately concluded that education could be the center of our campaign appeal. I am not sure we were willing to believe that the improvement of schools could be a winning issue. I wondered whether explaining our thoughts about more jobs, higher wages, economic development, and new industry would be more appealing to the voters. True, we get these things through education, but that is logic, and I wondered if enough people would see it that way.

I wasn't long in doubt. As I traveled over the state seeking support, prior to announcing, the audiences began to take the school issue away from me. "We must improve our schools" brought the most applause. The sensibleness of progress through education won the most favorable response at every stop. The newspaper editorials began to pick it up.

I talked about roads and farm income and industrial development and water resources, and the audiences were interested. I talked about schools and they clapped.

In a fairly remote county, one evening, a lady stood up to ask a question. She probably wasn't a heckler, but she sounded like one.

"Where are you going to get the money for all this stuff?" she demanded. I looked around the room and didn't see any newspaper reporters, so I decided to give her a blunt answer.

"Where do you think we will get the money?" I asked her. "From taxes!" The audience broke out in the best applause I had heard.

After we left I turned to Bert Bennett, who was scheduled to be my campaign manager.

"Do you realize what we experienced tonight? Voters applauded when I said we would get new school money from taxes. That's remarkable."

Bert laughed. "Yes, but I wouldn't be too sure. They thought you said you'd get the money from *Texas*."

But he and Henry Wilson agreed in seriousness that this was a dramatic development. Why not talk about taxes? Not only did the people understand the logic of school improvement, they appreciated the honesty of common sense. Of course better schools for our children would cost us more money. Why not make it a part of the campaign speech?

From then on we never failed to suggest the possibility of new taxes, and the promise never failed to get warm applause.

To lead the political battle for school improvement we decided to call on the women. I was sure women would add a fresh and lively touch to any election, and I believed they were idealistic enough to sense that we must make education the main thrust of the state. They were most likely to be concerned about the needs of the children. They were the ones who packed the children off to school every morning, and they were the first to feel the frustrations of weak schooling. They would never tire of this issue, and they wouldn't let the voters tire.

We set up a meeting in Greensboro of several hundred women immediately after the formal announcement of my candidacy. Doris Cromartie, Emily Preyer and Martha McKay, later Democratic national committeewoman, gathered them from all over the state, friends and friends of friends, many of whom had never before worked in a political campaign. I asked them to join our compaign forces, taking for themselves the assignment of getting across to the voters our education planks which I spelled out for them.

We would start with three principles, I promised.

First, improvement of education would have to be a long-range process; we couldn't continue to operate on a catch-as-catch-can basis from one biennial legislative session to the next, but would have to think in terms of at least ten years of constant improvement.

Second, public education, or at least its improvement, was primarily a state responsibility. We couldn't shove it off on the counties and cities, which too often lacked the money. Neither could we do nothing, inviting the federal government to enter the vacuum, and waiting for general federal aid which had been coming around the corner for at least twenty years to my own certain knowledge.

Third, our fundamental objective was quality education, the kind of quality that ensures that we are developing the capacity of children to think for themselves, the kind of quality system that would reach for the special needs of all the children.

"With the assurance that I do not imagine I am touching all the needs and possibilities, let me propose some points based on the principles. These points reflect the best thinking of school and legislative leaders. They will give us a good start. Likely we will want to add to them as we move along.

"1. *Teachers.* We need more teachers, and better qualified teachers. This means attracting capable people to the teaching profession and keeping them there. All other points are ultimately concerned with how to get good teachers and use them effectively.

"2. *Courses of Study.* First, we must be sure that we are teaching the basic subjects well. Next, we need the flexibility to prepare children according to their abilities. The gifted, the average, and the slower student obviously should not receive the same instruction throughout school. Courses should be carefully considered, to make sure that they are not shallow efforts in too many directions.

"3. *Constant Study of School Performance.* We need continuing research into methods, courses, techniques, teacher training, if we are to achieve constant improvement. We need to keep on asking how well are we doing, and how we might improve.

"4. *Money.* North Carolina's taxpayers have been getting their money's worth. The trouble is that they haven't been buying enough. The job cannot be done in a year, or two years, but we can, during a ten-year program, increase appropriations until we are able to get and hold enough qualified teachers.

"Talk about better schools would be hollow indeed unless a candidate is willing to mention the generally unpleasant subject of money. I promise that, if revenues are inadequate, I will have the courage to recommend additional tax sources to the General Assembly.

"5. *Buildings.* I believe that quality teaching is more important than buildings, but adequate facilities are needed. We do not need fancy frills, but we must have enough classrooms.

"6. *Recognition of Teacher Quality.* Subjective 'merit rating' has been found to be unworkable, but we need to evolve some way of rewarding exceptional teaching.

"7. *Smaller Classes.* Smaller classes are part of attracting quality teachers, because they relieve the drudgery and permit genuine teaching. They are part of quality education, because they allow the teacher to spend more time with each student.

"8. *Public Attitude.* To make the teaching profession a truly attractive one, we must provide an atmosphere that will show constant respect and concern for the teaching profession. It is not enough to show respect by an isolated act of belated public recognition for a long career of devoted service. We must show a continuing concern, not only through paying a salary commensurate with the service performed but through those added essentials to a feeling of dignity which all of us must have in order to give sustained peak performance.

"9. *A Well-rounded Economy.* Our hopes for the State are based on education first, supported by an improved industrial and farm economy."

Education was, of course, only one plank in a detailed campaign platform covering key issues ranging from agriculture to welfare, from atomic energy to water resources, and from race relations to recreation. But it was on this "quality education" plank that we built our hopes for the state's growth. This was the cause we assigned the women. They moved out from Greensboro to mobilize the women of the state. In every area, every county, they recruited crusaders for the schools. Every crusader received a booklet explaining the weaknesses and needs of education, and every booklet contained one hundred postal cards to be mailed to me, giving the name and address of each voter with whom the school issue had been discussed.

We had become convinced that the voters would respond to the call for a program to make our schools second to none in the nation, even with the possibility of higher taxes. As one newspaper commented, "That is a large order. But so was the educational dream of Charles B. Aycock sixty years ago. The people must be imbued with a vision of an ideal; they may never attain it, but let it still stand high in the sky to encourage the striving."

The elaboration of the education program during the campaign helped simplify the postelection task of developing specific legislative requests. However, even the campaign concept was not nearly specific enough to be a blueprint for action. We would also need to relate the concept to the budget, specified item by item.

The United Forces for Education played a major role in shaping a proposed budget. This organization is composed of the North Carolina branches of the American Association of University Women, the Congress of Parents and Teachers, the Federation of Women's Clubs including the Junior Women's Clubs, State School Boards Association, State Grange, and the North Carolina Education Association. The UFE believed that "Funds must be provided which will improve the instruction, guidance, and supervision of children; house them in safe, sanitary, and comfortable buildings; furnish them with a curriculum which is continuously evaluated and competently planned; and greatly increase the supply of qualified teachers."

They announced a $100 million enrichment program. I talked this over with Paul Thompson, my finance chairman, and Hugh Cannon, my law partner, and endorsed the entire UFE program the next morning. From that point on, the education issue belonged to us, and the other three candidates wasted much of their time attacking me as a big spender.

The UFE proposals were spelled out with almost budget-like precision. They called for:

1. An increase of approximately 23 percent in teacher pay; increases for all other personnel; salary adjustments for superintendents.

2. Extension of the teaching term by two additional days, so that the teachers might come in two days ahead of the arrival of the students.

3. Additional teaching personnel of 5 percent over the present allotment, eighty-seven assistant superintendents, sixty-five additional supervisors requested.

4. Clerical assistance for teachers and administrators.

5. Five days' sick leave for teachers.

6. Doubling of the library allotment.

7. Increasing instructional supplies by about 50 percent.

8. Establishment of in-service courses for professional improvement of teachers.

9. Increased salaries for college personnel.

10. Increased funds for Industrial Education Centers.

11. Increased allotment for school plant operation.

12. Adequate state matching for all available National Defense Education Act funds.

13. Additional teacher education scholarships.

14. Expansion of television teaching.

15. Establishment of a Department of Curriculum and Research.

16. Strengthening of the State Department of Public Instruction, by setting salaries on the basis of professional competence.

As the campaign continued, we talked about these things, and many more. May and June came, and after two primary elections, I was the Democratic nominee. I still had a difficult general election to face, but the budget-making machinery in North Carolina was in full operation. Although I had no official responsibility, this activity demanded my attention.

Our State Board of Education consists of ten appointed members, and three ex officio members, the Lieutenant Governor, the State Superintendent of Public Instruction, and the State Treasurer, all of whom are elected officials. The Board members are appointed by the Governor for overlapping eight-year terms, and traditionally are relatively free from direct political interference.

Along with all other agencies and institutions of state government, the Board of Education presents its proposed budget to an agency known as the Advisory Budget Commission. This commission consists of two gubernatorial appointees, along with the two senators and two representatives who served as chairmen of the two money committees, finance and appropriations, in the preceding session of the General Assembly.

The Governor and the Advisory Budget Commission then prepare a balanced budget based on estimated revenues and recommended appropriations. Our law requires that it be balanced. Under this arrangement Governor Luther H. Hodges prepared the budget which was to be presented by me to the 1961 General Assembly. This is an excellent system of fiscal management, because it gives continuity and provides budget recommendations which have been carefully weighed for more than a year. The Budget is printed in such a manner that the amount requested by any agency is shown on the same line as the amount set by the Advisory Budget Commission. Thus the legislator sees the complete picture.

In 1960 the Board of Education requested essentially the

recommendations of the United Forces for Education, calling for some $100 million in new funds in the biennial budget over and above the additional funds required by the increase in school enrollment. A request for this amount of new money was presented to Governor Hodges' Advisory Budget Commission, which in turn put about one third of these requests into the budget. That was all that could be done under existing estimated revenues. It was becoming painfully obvious that the time would come to call for new taxes.

Then from the budget hearing room I picked up the campaign trail again. The Republican party had a very fine nominee, Robert Gavin, who mounted a well-conducted campaign for himself and Richard Nixon.

The Vice-President swept into the state and presented a vigorous and appealing picture. It appeared that they had the best chance to win North Carolina since 1928, and after two hard campaigns we faced still another. There wasn't to be any coasting in, as often had been the situation.

I was growing weary of hearing myself talk about education, and I was afraid it might become a stale issue. I tried several other issues, but always school improvement brought the most responsive audience reaction. The people were determined that this was to be the main effort of the state.

It was late on election night when we breathed easy.

Now it was time to go to work.

I decided that first we would do all we could to bolster the secondary school system. This would mean that we were giving first attention to the average student, for he constitutes the bulk of the school population. This was the proper beginning point. Later we could turn our attention to education beyond the high school and to the specialized needs of certain children, such as the gifted, the retarded, the talented, the disadvantaged.

When, in February of 1961, the printed budget was handed to me for formal presentation to the General Assembly, a staff aide from the Budget Division sent over a suggested Budget Message dealing with each section of the budget. The public school section was described by the aide, in so many words, as "a good and forward-looking education budget." To that I added, in so many words, "But it is not good enough. We must provide all the money requested by the Board of Education, and I will prepare a second budget message with recommendations for the new tax sources which will be required."

Because during the campaign I had constantly reminded the voters of the possibility of new taxes, I was in a good position to claim a mandate as I faced the legislature. I had always hoped that rising revenues might spare me this unpleasant task. But they didn't rise fast enough. If we were to make significant school improvement, it had become inevitable that we seek additional taxes.

Even with the claim of a mandate, raising taxes is not easy. There was much opposition. We have in our political hierarchy a crowd known as the "hold-the-liners." They are opposed to anything that hasn't been done before.

They are opposed to taxes, too. All taxes. And they have much public sentiment running with them. It is, perhaps, indicative of how much we take schools for granted that parents who will seek out the best pediatrician for their child, buy toys and clothes far beyond any reasonable standard of need, and generally give their boy or girl the best they can possibly afford, will complain about paying taxes. Yet, taxes are the price of schools, and a good education is the greatest gift we can give our children. A child may be given every physical and emotional advantage at home, but for most of his waking day he is turned over to the school system, and it is odd that so many parents fail to understand that we can't afford to skimp on the quality of his teachers and equipment.

We had to have the new taxes. I talked with many advisers, and listened to all they had to say, but the basic decision had been made to ask for enough money to do the full job about which we had been talking. This was the only proper decision, but one full of political risks. Many of my close friends and supporters thought we ought not to try it. They reasoned that with rising revenues from the improved economy we could do enough to satisfy the public's expectations. They weren't sure the legislature would go along. Neither was I sure, but I knew we had to risk failure or forfeit an opportunity to lift the state to a new level of achievement. No one could deny that the real gain was worth all the political risks.

In March, 1961, I delivered my second budget message to the General Assembly. I asked it to remove all exemptions from North Carolina's 3 percent sales tax. This doesn't sound so bad when put that way, but the principal effect of removing the exemptions was to place the tax on food.

It seemed the fairest way, since we already had a modest income tax. It didn't seem burdensome because we ranked 49th in per capita taxation. Taxing so-called luxuries would not produce significant revenue. "Sin" was already taxed to the limit, although I did call for a 10 percent increase in liquor taxes. A tobacco tax would not bring in an adequate amount of revenue by itself, and with the sales tax we didn't need it. And there is no denying that we would have run into some high hurdles in a state that leads in both production and manufacture of tobacco products.

If we did not take the step, I told the legislators, inevitably the next administration would be forced to find new tax sources and we would have lost valuable time while avoiding no new taxes. We argued also that removing the maze of exemptions would give clean-cut tax administration. It has turned out that the merchant agrees. The new tax also, we contended, would provide a constantly rising revenue source to meet the constantly rising school population. It has. Also, this tax, it became obvious, was the only way in sight to improve the schools.

This change would bring about an estimated increase of $83 million during the biennium. I told the legislators we had to have it, and that the existing budget was totally inadequate to achieve the goals for public education which we had set for our state. I reminded them that we had many things to do, but the money had to come first.

I told them, "the quality we seek cannot be delivered by the General Assembly, although only you can start the march."

Selling a new tax, especially one that has been dubbed "the food tax," is not the easiest legislative task. Some members shook their heads and said, "You are going to wreck the Democratic party." Others thought we did not need to take such a giant stride all at once. "Can't we go just part of the way? Tax something else, not food." A few saw in its defeat a chance to embarrass me politically. Some insisted it was a regressive tax. In theory they were right. But we had to stand firm. There simply wasn't any other place to find the money.

Much of the reluctance was caused by the outcries of the constituents. Letters came to Raleigh and phone calls came to their homes. Characteristically, the opponents of any proposal are more vocal. Judge William Copeland, my legislative counsel, and I called on the friends of education, the local school boards, the citizens' committees, the PTA, to voice their support. After a few weeks the clamor at home was about equal pro and con.

Most of the reluctance came from the natural instinct to survive politically, an instinct found in all of us who seek political office.

A veteran of several terms, J. Henry Hill, Jr., expressed this fear, as did many of his colleagues. "You know I'll get beat if I vote with you, Governor. The Republicans about equal us in Catawba, as you know, and this is all they need."

"Oh, what do you care, Henry," I replied. "You're expendable."

He got a good laugh from this, promised his support, and every time I saw him he would laugh again and say, "I know. I'm expendable."

But he wasn't defeated. He has been re-elected every time since, and by better majorities than before.

About that time we were conducting a vigorous campaign to

raise $300,000 to bring home the battleship *North Carolina* as a war memorial and tourist attraction. We buttonholed everybody we could, from President Kennedy to lobbyists, and we commissioned as "Admirals" all who made a $100 contribution. We were seeking at least 2,500 Admirals. Herman West, Representative from Cherokee and a Republican leader, stopped at my office. He said he would like to be an "Admiral" and handed me $100.

"Nothing doing." I smiled. "That is, unless you will promise to vote for the tax." He did.

He showed his Admiral's Commission and told this story through all the lobbies. The tide was turning in our favor.

The 1961 General Assembly had the courage to vote this tax increase for support of public education, the largest that had ever been voted in the history of the state. The credit properly belongs to Lieutenant Governor Cloyd Philpott and legislators such as the finance committee chairmen, Senator Tom White and Representative Shelton Wicker, who fought day and night for the new school taxes, and the appropriations chairmen, Tom Woodard and Jim Stikeleather who skillfully shepherded through the budget items. Only one legislator was defeated in the subsequent election where the tax vote was made an issue. Surprisingly, the tax vote was not even an issue in most campaigns, and several who voted against the tax were defeated for that reason. The implicit lesson is that people will respond to the call for improving schools. Nobody likes taxes, but we are learning that ignorance is the most oppressive tax of all.

For months after the legislators returned home, the complaints continued. The check-out lines of the grocery stores were places of scolding remarks. Criticism of the tax outnumbered complaints about the weather. One store clerk told me about a lady, fresh from the beauty parlor next door, who was sharply unkind in her words about me and the 27 cents she was paying for "Terry's tax." She had in her grocery basket, among other things, 60 cents' worth of movie magazines, a six-pack of beer, about 50 cents' worth of candy, as well as a few groceries for her three children, two of whom would be going to their tax-supported school the next morning.

On the other hand, a local PTA group printed posters for grocery stores explaining how the tax pennies were being spent wisely for the education of the children.

One small group of critics, with considerable hullabaloo, started a caravan to buy groceries in a neighboring state. They made only one trip. They found that other kinds of consumer taxes in that state equalized the final price, but for a day they helped improve our roads by buying additional gasoline.

What did we do with the increased 1961 appropriation?

The new money raised the salaries of teachers and public school personnel by about 22 percent the very first year. It lifted supervisors' and superintendents' salaries about 30 percent. These increases were in addition to their regular increments.

To reduce the ratio of teachers to pupils, we increased teaching positions by 5 percent. In addition, the legislators approved the funds for forty-three more assistants for local superintendents.

The state library allotment per pupil was doubled, and the allotment for instructional supplies was raised by more than a third.

The new money provided an allotment for clerical assistance in local schools.

In-service training for the professional improvement of teachers was provided, and additional scholarship loans for teachers was authorized.

A curriculum study and research program was set up to keep the content and methods of courses current. An additional $200,000 was appropriated to conduct an experiment in merit pay for teachers.

Funds for the Industrial Education Centers were greatly increased, and the new money helped revitalize the vocational rehabilitation program. An appropriation was made to support state-level administration of the National Defense Education Program.

Higher education was not neglected. We were able to raise faculty salaries about 10 percent. We budgeted over a thousand new positions for the higher education system. State grants for community colleges were increased from $3.25 to $4.00 per student quarter hour of instruction.

The list of what was done with the money could be continued at some length, for every part of the school program received some benefit. There were more funds for educational television, and more for library books and journals at the colleges. The new tax produced tangible and significant results in every classroom in the state.

These things were bought with money, and money is essential, and getting the money was the difficult political action as far as the General Assembly was concerned.

But money isn't the most important reward for teaching. It is essential, but if it were the most important appeal we couldn't possibly attract the teachers with the money we pay or hope to pay. We need to move toward a decent and competitive salary range, but we need to do more.

What we pay reflects in an unspoken way how we regard the teaching profession and the teachers themselves. I suspect that we Americans, preoccupied as we have been for many years with the glitter of high salaries, the bonuses, and success as measured by the dollar, have failed to understand that many folks, including those who teach, do not necessarily have this materialistic gleam in their eyes. Lacking this understanding, we have been unable to tender our proper appreciation to them. Teachers covet a "fringe benefit," moreover, that titans of industry cannot provide: the special reward of the glow of recognition that lights a young face as it encounters and grasps new knowledge. They realize that the pursuit of money isn't all there is to life.

We have subconsciously downgraded the teacher because he

wasn't seeking wealth. And we have come back around the circle to the point where we conclude, collectively as the taxpaying community, that the teacher is not worth much of a salary because he doesn't know how to seek wealth and success, or he wouldn't be teaching anyhow. The fallacy has been our lack of understanding.

During the session of the General Assembly when I was trying to get enough votes to pass all the school appropriations we had requested, and later to obtain the necessary tax support, I had many discussions with the legislators. The questions varied, but, simply put, they all asked "Do we really need the money?"

We had a tradition in North Carolina that the Governor invites the members of the legislature to breakfast. The dining-room table seats about thirty, so with a few aides joining us, it takes about seven or eight days to include everybody. Over and over I invited them. Hardly a legislative day passed that I didn't have a group. The repeated discussions of the legislative school program were held against a backdrop of country ham, grits, red-eye gravy, scrambled eggs, fried apples, biscuits and sourwood honey. With a breakfast like this under his belt, it is hard for a legislator to be mean.

We would sit around the table, after eating, and discuss the numerous needs as spelled out by the budget items. Among other things, I contended we needed to pay higher salaries to teachers because we didn't have enough good teachers.

"Well," the answer came from some of the legislators, "why should we increase salaries for sorry teachers? You improve the teaching profession, require higher standards, establish a merit rating, and then we will raise the salaries."

In the first place, I answered, the great majority of teachers were entitled to much higher wages without delay. As for the rest, I argued that this was no chicken or egg dilemma; we knew which came first. Higher pay came first, and then improvement would follow. We had to start paying better salaries before we could start attracting better teachers. Of course, no one was in favor of rewarding incompetent teachers but, I insisted, "those who are incompetent will soon be moved out by the competition if we make the salaries more attractive."

Or the retort might be, "Surely you don't contend that paying a teacher more money will make her a better teacher." This would be answered in much the same manner, but the strange thing is that I have now observed that paying a teacher more money does make her a better teacher. At least the way we paid her had this result. We put teachers first. The legislative action indicated our official respect and esteem, in the very manner in which it was done.

It may very well be that the method of voting the school appropriations was the most significant part of the entire 1961 action. In former years it had been very natural to wait until the last few days of the session to determine the school budget. This was thought necessary because there were so many small requests for so many items from so many departments. The school budget always took some two thirds of the total budget, so it seemed appropriate to wait until the other items were voted in or out to determine how much was available for school improvement.

I decided as a matter of strategy that we would ask the joint appropriations committee to vote on the public school budget before they voted on any other part of the budget. The committee, made up of half the membership of the General Assembly, normally voted item by item on the recommendations it would make to the General Assembly, and the result of this voting generally was the final legislative decision. So, some weeks before the budget was to be voted into presentable form, our forces, without any warning, called for a vote on the public school section of the budget.

This was an unusual approach. The opposition rose up. About the only quick argument they could think of was to question "the wisdom of such a departure from custom," or they argued

"Let's wait to see if the finance committee is going to give us the money." The friends of education argued it was time to move forward. This was the showdown. The news reporters knew it. It was the story with the dramatic appeal. We were shooting it out at high noon. The vote was put and we carried it. Although technically the decision could have been modified or reversed later, this was not likely. If we had failed on this first tactical thrust, no doubt the entire effort of school improvement would have collapsed. We would have made some progress, but probably would have had to be content without the new taxes and the substantial improvement they would bring.

This action had considerable press coverage, and all the teachers and the school people and the patrons and the students knew we had finally put education first in the budget and had won.

During the campaign I constantly promised "to put education first," so this method of voting seemed to be a suitable way to show what we meant and how we measured its importance. There was another reason for calling for a vote under these particular circumstances. We were at stalemate. While the foes in appropriations argued "We don't know whether we will have enough money," the foes in finance were arguing "We don't know that we will need the money."

The joint finance committee, consisting of the other half of the membership of the General Assembly, was treading water. We needed the pressure of the additional appropriations to demonstrate that we did indeed require new tax sources to support the schools. So the favorable action of the appropriations committee put the leadership of the finance committee in a position to move. And move they did, maneuver by maneuver, step by step, beating down attempted crippling amendments and substitutes often with only a single vote to save us from being scuttled. But our side won. We had the taxes and we had the appropriations and we were on the road to considerable improvement.

The legislative budget placed the burden on individual teachers to do better jobs and almost all did. Even the highly competent continued to improve. Human nature responds to a wholesome challenge, and the challenge to improve our schools was clearly put into the hands of the teachers by the legislature.

I observed this over and over. Morale was much better, the spirit was much lifted, the teachers were working harder and were determined to do their part. They would "show" the legislature.

Statistically we didn't have too much to show. We moved from 39th only to 32nd in average salary of classroom teachers. However, the average teacher got an $831 salary increase that year, and that was almost $100 each month to remind the teacher of our regard and interest. We looked better in the ratings on per pupil expenditure, jumping from 45th to 38th.

This slow rise upward demonstrates how constant the struggle must be, as well as how far our neglect had let us fall behind. School improvement must be a year-after-year effort. In the year of these increases we had the added burden of just trying to keep up. We had over 60,000 additional students enrolled, requiring well over 2,000 new teachers just to stand still.

The college people told us that they immediately sensed an awakened interest in teaching majors, although it will take a little while to demonstrate this kind of change. We hoped that our emphasis on the teaching profession would result in heightening the interest of even the sixth and seventh graders in becoming teachers, as well as of those older and younger. We are able to demonstrate that elementary teachers graduating in North Carolina increased 33 percent from 1961 to 1964.

I could hardly go to a school over the next two years without a teacher seeking me out to say, "I came back to North Carolina because of the quality education program." Thus many of our exports, schooled initially at our expense, were being returned with additional training and experience at the expense of some other state. This was a direct and profitable return on our investment.

One principal told me that he had always dreaded to see August come, because he always found himself searching and scrambling for the last two or three necessary teachers. He would work out his needs, finally, by assigning an inept history teacher to teach mathematics or a physical education teacher to take care of the third grade. Always he had several teachers he didn't want to take, but he had to fill the slots. "This June," he reported happily, "I have my full teaching staff lined up and ready to go this fall."

Many other results are manifest in the reports of the Superintendent of Public Instruction. I reported to the incoming 1963 General Assembly by summing up most of the reports: "The most dramatic change has been the beginning of a new life in education. . . . Teachers are working harder, stretching for new ideas, doing a better job day by day, exhibiting a high morale and a higher sense of duty and dedication. . . . More consolidation, more improvement in courses of study, fewer dropouts, more dedication from principals, greater interest by parents, are positive signs of progress. Along with the emphasis by our State, there has been great new help from counties and districts, where ultimate responsibility lies."

I have listed most of the tangible results of the 1961 legislative action, and have mentioned the intangible results, but I am convinced that we would have obtained many of the intangible results even if we had lost the legislative battles. The point is that the political leadership was fighting, and fighting hard, for the improvement of the schools. The teachers and school personnel knew this, appreciated it, and would have supported the efforts to improve schools in other ways even if the money had not been immediately available. In any event, this is my thesis, but I am glad we didn't have to prove it.

Recently a governor of another state discussed with me an

impending fight with the teachers' association. They were threatening a strike or at least a demonstration. He didn't think this represented the thinking of most of the membership of the association, he wanted to improve his schools, but under his own particular circumstances he thought it was politically impossible to find new sources of tax money. I told him what an old legislator once told me: "If you can't give somebody what they ask, you can at least shed a little tear when you tell them you can't."

He could at least show his deep concern and could, as he did, start working on a widespread plan of school improvement, which in time would attract the necessary legislative support and financial appropriations.

So it has been my belief for a long time that the teachers not only are entitled to more money, they are entitled to more respect. They are entitled to respect in many ways: in public acknowledgment, in public position, in private and public appreciation. They are even entitled to more respect in the manner in which we provide more money for them.

I concluded that we must provide salary increases and advantages, such as smaller classes, and we must provide them in a gracious and not a grudging manner. We must provide them because teachers' contributions to society more than justify such consideration. We must provide them because in effect we are providing for our children, and the future of the community. We must provide them with the regret only that we could not have done more.

If a man looks around his community he will note, for example, that the doctor gets his proper respect and he gets it for saving lives. The teacher develops lives, and gives zest to life, and creates new life in terms of accomplishment. But somehow, by some inexplicable failure to comprehend, we have not thought this a very significant purpose.

I grew up in a little town in North Carolina by the name of

Laurinburg. We have our Confederate monument, as does every other county seat. But squarely in front of the courthouse is another monument. It was erected in 1905 to William Graham Quakenbush, and part of the inscription says:

Principal, Laurinburg High School
1879–1900

In recognition of his
exalted character
In appreciation of his
Ennobling influence upon youth
Erected by a people
grateful for his love and services

There is no monument for a lawyer, nor an accountant, nor a doctor, nor a merchant. This is symbolic of the kind of respect and appreciation the teacher is entitled to receive. While we cannot erect a marble monument to every teacher, we can show a heightened regard for the profession. This kind of recognition is a proper mark of the teacher's contribution to civilization.

CHAPTER III : It's More
Than Money

THE MORE I CONFRONTED the challenge of massive improvement of the entire education structure the more I realized that inertia was our foe. In North Carolina alone we needed literally hundreds of thousands of willing and working believers. Consider the thousands who make up the school committees, the school boards, and the boards of county commissioners. Add the tens of thousands who are the teachers, school administrators, and those who train our teachers. Then there are the parents, several hundred thousand, with varying degrees of interest, or disinterest, in and out of the PTA, but all supporting patrons of the schools at least to the extent of voting for those who provide the funds and make the decisions. There are well over a million students, and we would need at least a sprinkling of 10 percent or so as leaders to kindle the zest of the entire student body. This is quite an army, but not the kind that responds to direct marching orders.

I did not intend to try giving orders. A governor can get a highway built by writing a memorandum, but such a simple device will not lift the excellence of a school system spread across more than 50,000 square miles. For many reasons we needed to give far more people a sustained interest in education. For one thing, it was essential that the county authorities increase their own school supplements, rather than succumb to the human temptation to take the state money for use in place of their previous supplements. We would have made very little net progress if local money had been withdrawn.

One positive influence for greater local interest was the Curriculum Study, in which I. E. Ready had involved some 20,000 college and public school teachers with an equal number of laymen in almost every school administrative unit in the state. In addition we had the North Carolina Citizens Committee for Better Schools, first organized by Governor Hodges. Originally headed by Holt McPherson, and then by Richardson Preyer, with Raymond Stone as executive secretary, this group and the Curriculum Study stimulated interest in school improvement and paved the way for a promise I was to make.

In the fall of my first year in office, speaking in Charlotte to the teachers on their first day, I brought them all the appropriate exhortations. I also made a reckless statement. I got carried away and promised to visit every county to promote greater interest in schools. Having committed myself, I started a schedule of visits.

In a southeastern county, one of the first four visits I arranged, we had a decent little crowd together at the armory. It consisted of the school principals, the PTA presidents, a few school board members and county commissioners, a political friend or two, a delegation who came to catch me to talk about paving a secondary road, and a man who wanted me to parole his brother.

We had a good discussion, and the audience went away a little more dedicated and determined. But I realized I was missing the mark. These people already were sold on the need for improving their schools, and had been long before I had come onto the scene. We needed to do better.

The second meeting was about the same in composition. It,

too, was a morning meeting, and as we were breaking up to have coffee, L. A. Bruton, a principal, spoke to me. "Will you," he asked, "come to my school and talk to my student body? It is on your way and you will not be delayed ten minutes, and it will mean so much to my school." Even though my schedule was tight, what could I say? Of course, I would.

The response was warm and enthusiastic. I didn't make much of a speech, but asked them some questions and exchanged some quips. We talked as if we might have been together in a small group at the soda fountain. But I made the serious point that life would hold very little if they didn't make the most of school. I put the burden on them to improve their own school. They understood.

As I was leaving, shaking hands, I realized that I had never had a more responsive audience. Part of this undoubtedly was because, as the principal put it, "We have never had a governor visit this school before." It was something like seeing a big brown bear in the zoo.

But it was more than this. Children are generally more sophisticated and much smarter than we think, and they welcomed the challenge and the responsibility. They comprehended that the teachers could do so much more if the students wanted it done. They had the kind of pride that would ask, "Well, why shouldn't our school be the best in the land?" They knew enough and had seen enough to realize there was considerable validity to the suggestion that they, most of all, could improve the standards and the level of excellence. I also had a sneaking suspicion that they could have more influence on local officials, without deliberately trying, than any other group we might have running with us. It would be hard to deny students who were trying harder and were demanding better facilities and greater financial support.

Following this experience, we set up a statewide television program, announced as a special program for school students. I took about the same approach, informal, and with the same message. I asked students who understood and would help to write me. At a

IT'S MORE THAN MONEY

press conference the next day I made another reckless statement. I promised to answer them. Some 60,000 letters poured in. It took awhile, but I finally signed an answer to each one.

We then decided I would visit schools in every county, instead of arranging meetings to talk to leaders. We would invite the leaders to attend the school meetings, and we were sure they would get the message more clearly and loudly in this setting than in a sedate meeting scheduled just for them.

Whenever we could spare a day or so, we scheduled school visits. For the following three years we moved across the state, into every county, visiting a number of schools in the larger counties. One week I made fifty school speeches; on many days I made eight or ten, frequently ending the day with an evening speech to a teachers' meeting.

I remember particularly the day that John Glenn successfully orbited the earth. He was the first real American spaceman, and the children in the schools were fired with excitement. We made fifteen school visits that day, watching by television the preparations, the lift-off, and then the progress of the flight. As we moved from school to school I saw their anxious faces swept up in the new age, adding emphasis to the appropriateness and urgency of both our message and our program.

I believe that students will continue to carry on their important part of the school improvement program. They were directly involved, and they liked it. I know that I never got tired with all the traveling and speaking. Their response was always exhilarating. Their letters were always enthusiastic. I am counting on them to take a leading part in sustaining widespread public interest.

There are several other programs of general improvement of the schools which are worthy of some mention before we move on to higher education and the more specialized programs. Over a period of several years we considered carefully and logically the questions of merit pay for teachers. We set up a project for in-service training of teachers, including the use of television instruction. We carried forward a scholarship-loan program for prospective teachers. We re-examined our procedures of certification and our requirements of the teacher-training colleges. We promoted consolidation of the smaller schools with some degree of success. All these efforts were directed at the general improvement of the public schools, our first priority.

Merit Pay for Merit Teaching?

Teachers, while entitled to greater public respect and more generous compensation, nevertheless have no claim to immunity from criticism or improvement. Nor do they fancy that they have any such special privileges. They must try constantly to improve the job they are doing.

When a new legislator arrives in Raleigh, the odds are he will ask, "Why can't we pay teachers according to merit? Why do we regard those who intend to make it a career on a par with those who use it only as a temporary stopping place on the way to matrimony? Why is the pay the same for the able and imaginative teacher and a teacher who grits her teeth each morning with the fervent hope that she will be able to make it through the day until the last bell rings?"

These are valid questions. I asked them myself when I first came to the State Senate. The legislator soon finds that there is no simple answer when he starts trying to devise a detailed plan for merit pay.

In 1959 our legislature created a commission to explore the possibilities of paying teachers according to their performance. The report concluded that the principle was sound but cautioned that, since nobody knew how to grade teachers, we should do some experimenting before starting any drastic new methods of pay.

Accordingly, the next legislature authorized the State Board of Education to establish a pilot program and appropriated funds both for administration and for merit pay in the selected schools.

Merit pay for teachers has been and remains a controversial subject. While all will agree that a good teacher should be paid more than a mediocre one, it is difficult to find agreement about who is a good teacher, or to say who should rate his performance, and on what basis. At present almost every school district in the nation measures the level of teacher salary on the basis of training and experience. This type of single-salary schedule was developed about the beginning of this century.

Prior to that time a teacher's pay depended on what the school board thought she was worth. This method of individual negotiation led to unequal pay scales and to favoritism, as well as to other abuses both real and suspected. The single-salary schedule ended these kinds of problems, and has been fairly universally adopted.

There were many questions. Would such a plan create friction between teachers and principals, teacher and teacher? Is the principal or superintendent qualified or in a sufficiently free position to make a judgment involving such fateful consequences for the teachers? Do we evaluate the teacher's performance or her pupils' progress? How can the work of a teacher in an excellent school be compared with that of a teacher in a school where there are many "problem" pupils? Will parents be critical if their child does not have a merit teacher?

These many objections and questions indicated the wisdom of carefully planned experiments before adopting any widespread change of policy. It was quite possible that no change should be made. At least we would take a good and thorough look.

After a year of planning, three school systems were selected as pilot centers. These schools were in separate districts differing in size, location, and other factors which might influence the experiment. Altogether sixty schools and about 1,150 school personnel were involved.

It was agreed that it was essential for the teachers themselves to be brought in on the planning and that ratings would be restricted to those factors directly related to the teacher's responsibility. This program has been characterized by careful, intelligent planning, the use of local steering committees, with teachers, supervisors, and principals working as a team. There has been comprehensive evaluation. It may all come to nothing. The final report was made in April of 1965 and concluded that a just and workable merit pay structure could be established. The final recommendation was that there should be no state mandate, leaving the choice to local school boards.

In-Service Teacher Training

A schoolteacher, like any other professional, can get stale. At a recent dentists' convention I visited, most of the program was taken up with study courses and very little time was free for golf. Internal revenue people will approve this arrangement, but also the future patients will be benefited. The dentists know that there are constant changes and improvements in their profession, and this is one of the several ways they have of keeping up with developments.

In the 1961 session of the General Assembly funds for in-service teacher training were provided. The State Board of Education adopted procedures to enable local administrative units to organize institutes, courses, and workshops designed to improve the teachers' knowledge of their subjects. The success of this program is evidenced by the demand for considerable expansion, and also by widespread favorable reaction.

"I can already see more interest, as well as improved instruction in the subject fields, as a result of the art and social studies courses," one school official said.

Another commented that this program "has done more for the morale of teachers than any other single thing that has been done."

"Teachers discovered their weaknesses and resulting errors in speech and writing, and were motivated to continue to study in order to improve written and spoken communication" was the feeling of a principal.

The teachers liked it. "Why should a busy English teacher spend three hours a week studying world problems? Because it is my job to help the children I teach, not only to speak and write correctly but to have ideas and opinions to write about."

"In-service training is something that we need," another teacher felt. "If we do not stay ahead of our students, we are not teachers. We are only baby-sitters."

In the third year of this program almost 6,600 teachers took part in 213 local in-service programs, taught by instructors from 26 colleges. In one area, four summer institutes brought together 98 teachers. An in-service television study in modern math involved over 9,000 teachers, and in 1964–65, more than 14,000 teachers took part in this "keep-up" program. Most of the courses have been in social studies, English, and science, but the possibilities are at least as broad as the school curriculum. About half the courses were for college credit.

The overwhelmingly favorable response to the program indicated that teachers, like students, will welcome a chance to be challenged, to stretch their minds and the limits of their knowledge.

Relatively few teachers can afford all the summer training that is desirable. To be able to take a course with qualified instructors during the school year, in their own localities, adds a new dimension to our teaching force. The teacher who takes a course will do a better job not only because of what has been learned but because any kind of learning and study is stimulating. Perhaps just as important is the opportunity afforded the teacher to become a student again, and to see someone else standing in front of the class.

All we can do to improve the standing and standards of teachers will be our best investment. "The teacher is the seed corn of civilization. None but the best is good enough to use," is the idea expressed by Charles Duncan McIver, who worked with Governor Aycock at the beginning of the century to help the state break out of the bonds of illiteracy.

The importance of good teachers is one point on which all educators and critics agree. Admiral Hyman G. Rickover wrote that "The quality of an educational system depends wholly on the quality of the teachers . . . it may be doubted whether genuine reform of our schools is possible unless we acquire a new respect for teaching."

Professional study helps all professions. Our in-service helps make study available to a far greater extent for more people in more places.

Television in the Classroom

It is not at all likely that the teacher will ever be replaced by a machine, but many machines and devices are being used to assist in the job of teaching. Films are being used to bring ideas to life and to transport students to faraway places. These, along with filmstrips and slides, are rapidly becoming as essential as library books to a good school. They have demonstrated their worth.

Another of these "teacher aids" is television. There are people who dream that it will be possible for television to take on most of the teaching responsibility. It will not work out that way. Television will no more replace the teacher than textbooks did. Its use does pose many possibilities, but it is fair to say that at the present time no one has an exhaustive understanding of how these possibilities might best be exploited.

Much study has been carried on and North Carolina has done its part. With one of the original grants from the Ford Foundation, through the Fund for the Advancement of Education, we have learned many things. In 1964 about 30,000 students used the state's in-school television programs, despite the fact that these programs were limited to schools within the radius of one transmitting station. Some ten years ago the state, through the

University of North Carolina, acquired the license for Channel 4, and established educational television. In 1962 I created an *ad hoc* Governor's Commission on Educational Television to recommend the most efficient and fruitful ways in which the benefits of educational television might be provided for all the people in all parts of the state.

The 1963 General Assembly embarked upon a program of building enough additional transmitting stations, with additional assignment of channels, both UHF and VHF, so that our educational programs could be beamed to every corner of the entire state.

Educational television can supplement instruction in small schools; it can use a truly outstanding teacher to reach more students; it will permit teachers to spend more time with individual students. Beyond the classroom it can bring a history course to the housewife, and reading instruction to the illiterate. I am satisfied that all the demonstrated value of educational television will be enhanced constantly by imaginative development.

We are using television as a part of our in-service teacher training and have a series entitled *Methods for Modern Teachers*, shown after school hours, including such topics as "Creative Writing in High School" and "Motivating the Underachiever in the Regular Classroom."

Since our circuits are not closed, there will be many side benefits for the public at large. One mother wrote: "Whenever possible I turn on your program. Your stimulating presentations not only help make up a deficit in my own education, but make a point of contact with our teen-age sons."

Loans for Future Teachers

We are attempting to attract more teachers in other ways. In 1957 North Carolina established a scholarship-loan program for prospective teachers. Scholarships are awarded on the basis of academic ability, financial need, personal qualifications, interest in teaching, and the statewide shortage of teachers in the applicant's field of major interest.

The scholarship, or loan, is $350 a year for four years, with $350 to be forgiven for each year the recipient teaches in a North Carolina public school. If the student does not fulfill these teaching requirements, the loan is to be repaid with 4 percent interest.

The need for teachers makes this a sound public policy. My only reservation is that the amount of the loan is too small, and the number of scholarships too limited. For the 600 scholarship loans available in 1964 we had 2,100 applicants, at least half of whom were clearly qualified. The next step is to expand this proved program. We could use 2,000 loans of at least $500 each year.

Teaching Teachers

Certification of teachers, how they are taught, what they are taught, have long been subjects of discussion. "She ought not to study so much about how to teach; she ought to be learning what to teach." James Bryant Conant made this subject the basis of careful study, concluded with some valid criticisms, and suggested some constructive changes.

There is something to be said for both sides. Some schools of education have required too many meaningless courses in methodology, wasting valuable time with needless repetition. On the other hand, I have had the firsthand experience of being bored to death by accomplished scholars who knew not the first thing about presenting the subject matter in which they were so creditably accomplished.

At college the student can overcome this inadequate teaching, and can read the scholars' books, and indeed maybe this kind of academic presentation is good discipline. But in the lower grades the teacher, whatever her knowledge, needs all the skill she can muster to get across the lessons she must teach. It never has seemed to me such a difficult problem to surmount. It is, after all, a matter of balance. We need the best of both.

In 1962 the State Board of Education adopted an "approved program" approach to teacher education and certification, which gives public and private teacher-training institutions greater responsibility in determining that candidates for certification are properly prepared.

Institutions desiring approval submit applications and reports of self-studies to the State Department of Public Instruction. If these appear to meet guidelines for resources, faculty, personnel policy, curriculum, and facilities, a state committee visits the institution to interpret and evaluate the report.

This committee's findings are then reviewed by a State Evaluation Committee on Teacher Education, which submits its recommendations to the State Board of Education. The State Board may then approve the institution for a period up to five years. Each institution must re-evaluate its program every five years, and submit at these intervals to the established procedures for visitation and approval.

A part of the requirements deals with the selection of students. The burden is placed on the institution to recruit, select, and retain for teacher preparation only those students who show promise of becoming successful teachers.

This program puts the burden where it should be, on the institution doing the training, but it sets broad standards, carefully evolved, generally conforming to those of the National Council for the Accreditation of Teacher Education. It allows flexibility, but requires constant self-evaluation.

The potential danger is that we will lapse into carelessness and allow the established guidelines to become the maximum achieved. It is also possible that the guidelines will be developed too rigidly, discouraging fresh approaches. If we can avoid these dangers, placing this new responsibility on the teacher institutions should improve teaching.

Consolidation of Smaller High Schools

Even if better college courses turn out better qualified teachers, we will continue to miss the mark of excellence in a school system that is inadequately organized. Consolidation of small schools into larger, more useful schools is a stubborn, prideful problem. It is quite possible for a high school to become too large, losing some of its feeling for the individual student. I can cite a few examples. It is much more likely, however, that the student will suffer if the school is too small. Consolidation is a decision that under our law, and properly so, must be made locally. However, I never failed to encourage consolidation of small high schools.

One dedication ceremony I attended was for a new consolidated high school that had brought together, by a local bond issue, six small high schools. It served the southern part of a fairly large county. It was well designed and spanking clean. There were parents there who had opposed the merger because "You're taking the heart out of our community" or "I don't want my children to spend most of their time riding buses." These former dissenters were obviously proud of what they saw; everybody was.

More important than the building was the new opportunity it brought with it. Here now, with an adequate number of students, there could be a broadened curriculum, offering more courses, a wider choice for the students, with more teachers.

I wandered around the building, escorted by two high school students in crisply fresh new dresses. We went into the modern chemistry laboratory, the first these students had ever seen except the one at the old school which contained a couple of Bunsen burners and a pickled frog in a jar. At their new school they had three laboratories, containing invitations to mysteries they never even knew existed.

More important than the laboratory was the teacher I found there. He was a mature young man. He had taught in Florida for nine years, had been visiting friends, was impressed by the building and equipment, the spirit he found for school improvement, and had applied for the job. There he was, a rich dividend for all the efforts of the community.

The library was well designed, and well stocked, and by coincidence the librarian had also come from outside the state. It was the kind of library that made the eyes of this young professional sparkle. She had worked in a small library, long neglected, where the typical works were Stevenson's *A Child's Garden of Verses*, purchased in 1931, and *Ivanhoe*, contributed by the widow of a local doctor. Now she had the place, the books, the children. I have never seen a more enthusiastic young teacher. She said that she would have "gladly have taken a cut in salary to have this opportunity, but I'm getting all this and a raise too."

Such are the unmeasured benefits of consolidation.

CHAPTER IV : What About the Talented?

ONE EVENING John Ehle and I were talking about some of the special needs and the special challenges and he asked a question. "Why don't we find a campus and set up a resident school for high school students who have unusually high academic ability?" We haven't done it yet, but born of that idea were some other new approaches to public education.

John Ehle is a novelist. He has written fiction and nonfiction such as *Shepherd of the Streets*, *The Land Breakers*, and *The Free Men*. He was at Chapel Hill when I first knew him, teaching in the department of Radio, Television and Motion Pictures, at the University of North Carolina. Through common friends he had suggested several good ideas to me. He had just published a newspaper article which lambasted what he termed the university's sterile approach to the teaching of the arts. While there were at least two sides to the question he argued, nevertheless here was a man willing to call for a fresh approach. I was considerably impressed.

My legal assistant, Joel Fleishman, told me one day that Ehle was about to take a sabbatical leave and would be in New York working on another novel. Joel thought he could do more good in North Carolina and that we should invite him to spend his year working in state government. Earlier I had attempted to lure a retired college president to work with us in presenting ideas to private foundations, but had been unsuccessful. The idea of using Ehle's abilities appealed to me. I was sure that he would more than earn his keep.

I invited John Ehle to dinner and he stayed two years. His first year's salary was obtained from the Richardson Foundation. If I were to write a guidebook for new governors, one of my main suggestions would be that he find a novelist and put him on his staff.

By the end of my first year in office we had started many things which, if carried forward and developed, would benefit the average student. The continuing school visits dramatized our concern for all students and our determination to raise the quality of our public schools. Now we had time to turn our attention to trying some new things.

North Carolina had already started considering a statewide program to challenge the gifted student to more excellent accomplishment. The 1959 General Assembly had authorized a commission to study the education of exceptionally talented children. The neglect of these students had been one of our most needless wastes of human resources. True, many were outstanding without any additional motivation or specialized programs. But too many simply took school as they found it, drifting along with little effort and consequently little development. This waste, I think, was at the core of the criticisms advanced by Admiral Hyman C. Rickover. While I recognize why many school people bristled at some of his suggested methods, he made the point that we were not achieving the excellence we would require for survival.

Today in America there are many notable programs for these

children. A vast body of literature has grown up on the subject. Public acceptance of such programs has spurted forward since 1956 when the Educational Policies Commission of the National Education Association favored some special groupings and acceleration but expressed concern about possible personality damage to the child. Personally, I quit worrying about personality damage after hearing the students at our special summer school sing a theme song they had made up, joshing themselves, the chorus of which was "O we is gifted, we is gifted."

Now the National Education Association has a "Project on the Academically Talented Student" and furnishes schools information to help set up special programs. The Educational Policies Commission of the NEA summed up the current thought: "Gifted pupils should be identified early and given early opportunity to challenge their powers and develop their talents to the fullest. They should be motivated to high achievement and should have a sense of responsibility for the wise and socially profitable employment of their abilities." How can this be done? There will be many approaches.

The chairman of our commission was Dr. C. D. Killian, head of the Department of Education at Western Carolina College. He had done pioneering work conducting summer programs for gifted children, which not only produced significant improvement during the summer but developed new skills which the students retained on returning to their own schools.

In attempting to come to some sensible recommendations, we found that the diversity of North Carolina added to the difficulties. If 5 to 10 percent of students fall into the talented category, what do you do in a school with 300 students in all grades as contrasted with a school of 1,400 in the high school grades alone? What do you do in a county of 300,000 that can be applied in a county of 16,000 population? Is it best to group all these students with unusual talent in one place, or should you catch them where they are? Nobody knew, and nobody knows, but our commission took the wise approach of recognizing that any North Carolina plan must have flexibility.

The General Assembly assigned the commission the task of determining the best methods of identifying talented children and the best method of training to develop their endowments.

At the outset no one knew the extent or nature of what was being done for North Carolina's gifted, so first the commission invited all principals to describe practices established for the talented in their schools, including identification, testing, special materials, and organization. This inquiry was a bit shattering for principals who had given no thought to such a program. The inquiry not only furnished important data for the commission; it started principals thinking more about what they could and should do. It was found that 368 elementary schools and 214 high schools were already attempting to do something for pupils of superior mental ability, but "these local programs certainly need consulting services and support from the state."

Our commission's research consisted mostly of action studies, with pilot centers set up in different parts of the state, in rural, urban, large, and small schools. These were designed to demonstrate possible procedures, such as nongraded primary classes, special classes, itinerant teachers. Additional study of programs already operating enabled the commission to present a program tailored to North Carolina's needs.

On the basis of the commission's work, the 1961 General Assembly set up a state program for the talented. It established criteria for identifying the gifted, provided for a staff within the State Department of Public Instruction, and appropriated funds for teachers in approved programs. The local schools were given the opportunity to present programs for the talented, and, if acceptable, the state then provided the funds for the teachers.

The types of programs actually offered include special elementary classes, with emphasis on depth and enrichment; special instruction for a regular period in subjects in which the child is ahead of his regular grade level; itinerant teachers who work with several schools; and advanced placement classes.

In Winston-Salem, one of our largest and best systems, there has been developed a comprehensive and successful program beginning with the third grade. Students are selected after incisive mental and psychological evaluation, and assigned to self-contained classes. They use state-adopted texts merely as springboards to broader explorations of the subjects.

In the Winston-Salem junior high schools these students are grouped into "common learnings" classes for most of their time. For example, one class of seventh-graders centered their activities around the subject of better world understanding. This involved them in studies in depth of the literature and history of many nations. The rest of the student's time is spent in regular courses, but with wide discretion about when a student is ready for a particular subject. In senior high school the qualified students are permitted to enroll in small advanced study classes. The parents also are given the benefit of special seminars.

The Winston-Salem program was directed by Douglas Carter, a bright young teacher with an unusual appeal for students, and later we drafted him to help run our Governor's School.

The Winston-Salem approach obviously wouldn't work in a smaller school system. Mitchell County, for example, has about 3,500 students in its elementary and high schools. There are nine schools in the county, so an itinerant teacher is used to visit the schools several times a week and teach a group of exceptionally talented children. The students are taken out of their regular classrooms and given instruction in areas that are not part of the regular program. In the 1961–62 school year there were 64 full-time teachers for exceptionally talented children, with over 2,000 students. Two years later more than 10,000 students were involved, and for the fall of 1965 preparations have been made for 25,000 students to be enrolled in some program for the gifted. Thus, results were immediate.

Our school people are well aware of the need for constant re-evaluation. There are no inflexible state rules. As two national experts put it, "Research findings on this problem, however, are in conflict. Furthermore, it is difficult to generalize research findings from one community or school and apply them to the practical situation in another . . . educators will be wise to put aside, as much as possible, long-standing traditions and biases and look anew at the problem."

We wanted to find a way to do some research of our own, and we wanted to glamorize superior academic efforts by superior students. So we put part of John Ehle's idea into being.

This was to be a summer school for rising juniors and seniors from the high schools of North Carolina. The student body of 400 was to be selected from those students with superior ability and performance or unusual artistic ability. There would be no charge to the student, so selection could be on merit alone.

At Salem College, in Winston-Salem, President Dale H. Gramley was willing to let us use his campus during the summer months. The Carnegie Corporation thought it such a good idea that it put up half the money required for a three-year period. The businessmen of Winston-Salem agreed with Carnegie, and put up the other half, for a total budget of $450,000.

The State Board of Education called it the "Governor's School" and opened the first session in the summer of 1963. We wanted to see what gifted students could do and learn in an unlimited academic environment. For eight weeks the challenges to unleash their minds were laid before them and all around them. For most of the students this was a completely new approach to education, and their response was overwhelmingly favorable.

One girl from Linwood, North Carolina, wrote to the director of the school:

"I can hardly find words to express what I want to say. The words I do find will be frightfully inadequate.

"Firstly, thank you so very much for writing my letter of

recommendation to Smith College. As you have probably read in the paper, I received a $2,100 scholarship . . . This was a miracle, and if I didn't believe in them, I do now. . . .

"But most important, I thank you for my two summers at the Governor's School. I am becoming increasingly aware that you and the Governor's School are responsible for the benefits I am reaping now. The Governor's School is responsible for my getting to study with inspiring teachers, for my being really introduced to the Humanities, for my meeting such absolutely grand people, many of them lasting friends—for so many things, most of them ineffable. Most important of all, your Governor's School is responsible for my downright *joy* for learning."

Each student spent eighteen classroom hours a week in his major-interest areas: mathematics, English, French, social sciences, natural sciences, art, choral music, instrumental music, or dance and drama. Each spent three hours in a minor area and four hours in a class of "Essential Ideas."

The drama students, the first year, performed *Twelfth Night* and portions of other plays ranging from *Electra* to *The Importance of Being Earnest,* and always to capacity audiences of Winston-Salem people. There was a symphony, a choir, and an art show of the students' works.

There was plenty of recreation, plenty of athletic activity. A number of the boys had earned their athletic letters. This was a well-balanced group. No grades or credits were given. There were no tests or assigned homework, as such. But the students worked harder and longer than they ever had before. They read widely and well, and were allowed to take some books home with them, as a start toward a personal library.

Some 3,000 teachers have visited the school at the invitation of the Board of Directors. Each group is given a morning orientation program and spends part of the day observing the students and the teachers in action. The response of these teachers, as well as those who have taught in the school, give some indication of its impact on the state:

A California professor, who wanted to teach high school for a summer, said, "If we could only do this with students like these for nine months, the result would be almost beyond imagination."

A visiting observer-teacher compared the school to her classroom and noted that "the atmosphere here is definitely more stimulating and conducive to exploratory thinking. The students were more eager to involve themselves and probe the depths of their thinking."

The school was directed by the State Board of Education and by an Advisory Board consisting of Virgil S. Ward, J. E. Miller, and I. E. Ready. It has a Board of Directors, of which Henry H. Ramm is chairman. Mr. Ramm is vice-president of R. J. Reynolds Tobacco Company, and was the chairman of the luncheon of Winston-Salem firms and foundations that raised the money to match the Carnegie grant. Incidentally, this took less than fifteen minutes. He and Charles H. Babcock, another community leader who has helped us in a number of projects, had laid the necessary groundwork.

The superintendent of the school is Joseph M. Johnston who, in his spare time, is Supervisor of Curriculum Development in the State Department of Public Instruction. The principal and program director is C. Douglas Carter, director of special programs for the Winston-Salem schools, who has a special talent for making boys and girls come alive.

Salem College is located in Old Salem, which was originally settled by Moravians in 1766 and has been restored to its eighteenth-century appearance. It is a major tourist attraction, and may be unique in that most of its sixty-four original buildings are still habitable. Exposure to this kind of setting was itself a stimulating experience to youngsters from remote or small towns, or even crowded cities.

The work done, the aftereffect, the methods of motivation, the tempo of learning, and all other aspects are being carefully studied and evaluated by a number of people and institutions, including the Learning Institute of North Carolina. This indeed is a laboratory of learning which should demonstrate useful lessons for the entire school system. It was our intention that it serve that purpose, as well as constituting the capstone of a statewide program of providing additional challenges for students capable of superior accomplishment.

There have been many letters and editorials and personal evaluations from the students themselves about the meaning of this school. The goal of the school was expressed by a mother, who wrote, "The privilege of attending the Governor's School has been the finest thing that ever happened to Tom. . . . As the days pass, he is sharing more and more of his summer experience with us. When asked what he had learned he hesitated, then said, 'It is hard to tell—but this I know, I want to learn now more than I have ever wanted to in my life.' "

Everybody was amazed at the artistic talent that was discovered. I expected the academic ability. I was not entirely prepared to find the unusual artistic talent. And I kept thinking how much more there must be in the towns and villages of North Carolina. At the end of the summer a little girl, who I am told has unusual musical talent, wrote me, "Being from a small town, I had never attended concerts or drama and dance productions. I realize what I have been missing, and I intend to make every possible effort to go to Charlotte where these are frequently presented."

We were doing a number of things to promote the development of the arts, but our experience with the Governor's School stimulated doubts about whether we were beginning to do enough.

North Carolina government had been active in support of the arts, perhaps as much as any other state. The state sponsors the North Carolina Symphony Orchestra, directed by Benjamin F. Swalin. We doubled the state appropriations, and instituted a subscription Symphony Ball at the Governor's Mansion each year to provide additional funds. In 1964 the orchestra played in 54 communities, and also gave free concerts for 152,000 school children.

The outdoor drama had its modern day beginning in North Carolina. The state has sanctioned and provided some support for Kermit Hunter's "Horn in the West" and "Unto These Hills," and Paul Green's great drama "The Lost Colony," which has now played each summer for more than a quarter of a century.

All these furnish education in the arts. So does the North Carolina Art Museum, to which thousands of school children come each year, as do thousands of older citizens, to view the original paintings representing all the great ages. North Carolina was the first state in the Union to appropriate tax money—$1 million—to purchase art. This appropriation, right after World War II, was matched by a gift from the Kress Foundation. Today its more than a thousand works are valued at more than $7 million. North Carolina has made all its people the owners of a collection to rival that of a Medici prince, which is completely appropriate for a democratic government.

North Carolina also has established a State Arts Council, and has advanced the arts in a number of other ways.

In the summer of 1962 I attended for a weekend the Transylvania Music Camp, in the mountains of Western North Carolina at Brevard, which is one of the best in the country and draws students from all over the South. The state provides a negligible part of the cost. Sitting on the porch of the lodge on Sunday, eating a picnic lunch with the director and founder of the camp, James Christian Pfohl, and Mrs. Pfohl, we talked about his students and their opportunity to develop their talents.

"Why," I asked him, "do we not have a music conservatory like the Juilliard in North Carolina, or somewhere in the South?"

"Because," he said, "nobody ever started one."

Would it go? Is it needed? Could we get the students? His answers were enthusiastic. Of course it is badly needed. Of course we would get the students. We have more talent than any other part of the nation and we need to provide greater opportunities for its development.

On the way back to Raleigh I wrote out a directive setting up a study commission. "Look into the possibilities of a music conservatory in North Carolina which would be organized to serve this entire region. Where should it be located? What would be the costs? How should it be organized?"

I appointed a group of knowledgeable citizens, with Mrs. Martha Muilenburg of Charlotte as chairman. Actually, this was another part of John Ehle's idea, so I assigned him to bird-dog the committee.

The committee collected basic facts and figures, sought the advice of arts leaders, and turned in a report which gave me almost more than I had bargained for. Yes, said their unanimous report, we need a music conservatory, but we need more than just that. In addition, we need a residential high school.

The report was thorough. It concluded that, while music instruction was offered over the state, it was generally difficult to find sufficient talented performers in any one place to make up a group large enough to warrant a professional teacher. For this reason a residential school was required. There was only one residential high school of performing arts in the nation, the Interlochen Academy in Michigan, a private school which had just opened. New York City had a public high school of Music and Art, which opened prior to World War II, but it had no need for residential facilities.

In the meantime John Ehle had called on a national foundation and had taken me to New York to see the proper person, who expressed considerable interest, provided we had a "going concern." I understood his reservations, and I felt reasonably certain that we could get going.

But was this the approach? I sent the report to a number of performing artists and asked their opinions. The response was more than encouraging. All these very busy people not only took time to read the report but were uniformly enthusiastic. José Limón wrote that the committee's creation "is to me no less than a triumph for the forces which create culture and civilization and nurture and elevate the human spirit, and by which a city, state, region or nation is known, understood and remembered." Elia Kazan pointed out that America was far behind the rest of the world in the development of the arts and expressed the hope that the school could coordinate with the Lincoln Center Repertory Theater as a "sort of cousin" in the community of arts. Martha Hill, director of Juilliard's dance department, commended this effort toward decentralization of the arts, saying that "to build for the future, opportunity in the arts must not be confined to the largest cities in the country."

There were many cogent suggestions about the pitfalls, and many helpful questions. The curriculum should emphasize performance and concentrate on the practice of the particular art. The school should be in a city capable of supplying audiences. There should be no compromise with excellence.

So we had the plan, and we had the encouragement, and now we had to find the best way to get the program started.

I thought we should go to the General Assembly, because I believed the school should be a function of the state. Furthermore, it was doubtful that we could get much foundation help unless we did take the first step and put the school into being.

But there was contrary advice. The General Assembly was in session at the time, and this item had not been included in the budget. It would have to be presented as a supplemental bill, which meant that it could not be considered until after the regular budget had been passed. This would put it awfully close to the end of the session. Neither did we have the advantage of a precedent to hold up to the legislators. No other state was supporting such a school. Some advisers thought that the legislators would feel that it was not a worthy project, and surely not a necessary one.

It was certain that if we went to the legislature and failed we would eliminate all hope of foundation support. The plan would be dead.

I decided to take the chance. I remembered a response John Motley Morehead had made to critics who, when he gave the University of North Carolina a multimillion-dollar planetarium, complained that he should have provided instead for some of the more essential building needs. "Let the legislature mend the University's pants," he told them. "I am going to buy it a new top hat." I had a hunch that when the legislators had finished mending the state's pants they would be willing to buy a top hat. We went to the legislature.

It was my practice to assign responsibility for each administration bill to a member of the executive branch of the administration. We do not operate with floor leaders as many states do, and while we had many leaders in the legislature we had all agreed this method of assignment was a good practice. I called in Ben Roney, Director of Secondary Roads, and told him I had a tough one but I thought he could get it through. "Okay," he said, "but I think I should tell you I have already heard your enemies call it 'the toe dancing bill.' "

Senator Ralph Scott and Dr. Rachel Davis, a Representative, introduced the bills. Public hearings were held. It was discussed in committees and debated on the floor under the able leadership of Representative David Britt. Our proposal was that spending the state money would be contingent on getting private matching funds. We thought we had the votes but were afraid it was close, and experience had taught us that a bill of this kind could fly all to pieces in the face of crippling or humorous amendments. As the House debate progressed one well-educated representative spoke forcefully against the proposal. "I just don't think we ought to spend money to learn people to pick banjers and toe-dance," he said in mockery.

Another said that if his son were to mention ballet to him he'd send him to another institution—a mental institution. There was

also opposition from a few colleges, where there was fear that the
school might detract from existing programs by siphoning off the
top talent from all over the state. This position was stated in
debate.

Then there rose for recognition our venerable veteran cur-
mudgeon, John Kerr, a former Speaker of the House, whose
support of the administration had been nothing like consistent
and whose vote Ben Roney had not counted. He had ridiculed
many a bill to death in his generation of service. What would he
say?

John Kerr, like most of us, has his failings, but he is an
aristocrat in the pure definition of the word. His forebears date
back to colonial days. This was a cause natural to the spirit of an
aristocrat. He understood fully the meaning of the arts to a
civilization. His speech was the most eloquent of the entire
session: ". . . the beauty and glory of Ancient Greece have not
faded one iota. . . . Why shouldn't we take the leadership in
this . . . let's build something for the future . . . this is North
Carolina's next venture in an age of intellectual development."
. . . He ridiculed, but he ridiculed the opponents of the bill.

"There may be toe dancing," he concluded, "but if there is I
want to be in the audience."

The bill passed by the surprising margin of 80 to 18. It also
passed the Senate by an equally safe margin. The sum of $325,000
was appropriated, contingent on obtaining matching private
funds. The bill set up a "school for the professional training of
students having exceptional talents in the performing arts" under
a twelve-member board of trustees, appointed by the Governor
for overlapping terms. Dr. James Semans, of the faculty of Duke
University Medical School, is chairman. The State Department of
Public Instruction will have jurisdiction over the academic curriculum, just as it does for other high schools. The Board of
Higher Education will be concerned with education beyond the
high school.

An Advisory Board for the school was authorized, to which I appointed Sidney Blackmer, a North Carolinian, as chairman, and with him conductor Dr. James C. Pfohl, writer and teacher Paul Green, choreographer Agnes De Mille, composer Richard Adler, dancer José Limón, composer Peter Mennin, conductor Julius Rudel, composer Vittorio Giannini of Juilliard and the Manhattan School of Music, actor José Ferrer, Madame Eugénie Ouroussow, executive director of the School of American Ballet, and singer Jan Peerce. Their enthusiastic acceptance of the assignment is an indication of the reception of the idea of such a school by performing artists.

The Advisory Board visited the four cities which had made bids for the school, and recommended Winston-Salem where a thirty-acre school site with adequate classrooms, auditorium, and gymnasium had been made available. Also, Winston-Salem citizens, sparked by Smith Bagley and Philip Hanes, in a 48-hour campaign, had pledged a million dollars for dormitories. So Winston-Salem is the location. Special trustees, headed by Winston-Salem businessman R. B. Crawford, were appointed to obtain and disburse the private funds which are expected.

The Advisory Board suggested the name "North Carolina School of the Arts," and recommended that Vittorio Giannini be elected president. Professor Giannini established his residence in Winston-Salem, recruited the finest possible faculty, and opened his school in September of 1965.

Artists from all over the United States began to catch the enthusiasm of the first state-supported school of the arts in America.

Andrés Segovia, the famous classical guitarist, agreed to give master classes at the school, and as an indication of his faith in what we were trying to do, donated a portion of his fee for guitar scholarships.

In addition, Segovia nominated Jesús Silva, his outstanding student and protégé, to serve as a resident professor of guitar.

"Silva is one of my favorite students," he said. "But that is a thing of the past. Today, he is a conscientious teacher, a scholar, and an artist."

And from the North Carolina hills and the Tennessee mountains came the guitarists and banjo pickers . . . for pickin' and singin' is a grand art in the mountains. And on the first day of auditions, Jesús Silva, young protégé of the man who revived the guitar as a concert instrument, heard this raw talent and noted dryly on one of the applications, "uses pick . . . needs instruction."

The auditions represented the crucial moment in the life of the school. The legislature and the foundations had given it breath; the city-county school board had released Gray High School to house it; the people of Winston-Salem had contributed a million dollars for its sustenance; Dr. Giannini had convinced a dazzling faculty to serve the idea.

But all of this had been done on faith—the faith that there were boys and girls in North Carolina and the South whom God had blessed with talent to grow as artists if given the encouragement, the stimulation, and the outlet. More than five hundred boys and girls came from all around the state and the South and a few from across the country to the auditions. In North Carolina we had set up a network of volunteer talent scouts in almost every county.

Former Metropolitan soprano Rose Bampton and bass-baritone Norman Farrow held the auditions in voice; Olegna Fuschi and Howard Aibel on the piano; Marc Gottlieb, first violinist with the Claremont Quartet, in strings; Saul Caston, former conductor of the Denver Symphony Orchestra, in timpani and brass; Robert Listokin, clarinetist with the Clarion Quintet, worked with the woodwinds; William Trotman, Bentley Anderson, and William Ball directed drama, with the help of Mr. and Mrs. Sidney Blackmer, who flew in from New York to be present.

Robert Lindgren, who danced with the Ballet Russe and the

New York City Ballet, became the head of the dance department and invited ballerina Alexandra Danilova, his former dancing partner now with the School of American Ballet in New York, to assist him with the dance auditions. The auditions consisted of two parts: a free form solo, in which the student selected his or her own composition and style, and a formal class, with the two instructors putting the aspirants through their paces at the bar.

One girl from Lincolnton performed her free form and was described by Lindgren as "possessing an animal grace . . . a natural dancer." Yet she was helpless during the formal instruction and seemed to wander about and lag behind. Finally, she admitted to her instructors that she had never had a lesson and had learned all that she knew from watching television. I don't know whether it is true, but it is rumored that Lindgren then turned to Danilova and said, "This is what the school is all about. This girl must be accepted."

The parents suffered terribly during the auditions, for they had to sit outside while their sons and daughters went to try out. Messages would filter down from time to time, like, "Mr. Aibel and Miss Fuschi were beside themselves over a little pianist from Selma, North Carolina, who plays like Mozart"; or, "Rose Bampton says she has just heard a voice with the promise of greatness."

When the tensions and the tears were over, and some were chosen and some were not, Giannini said, "The auditions more than confirmed our faith that the school can serve a great purpose. For so many children, who cannot afford private instruction, the school is a godsend.

"Certainly, not all are geniuses. In the arts, many are called and few are chosen. But that is not the point. The joy on their faces makes the weariness and the headache all worthwhile."

Giannini went on talking about the artists who had left New York and elsewhere to come to North Carolina and give their time, many commuting at great inconvenience to themselves.

"It is the idea of the school. Every artist knows what good

Photo by Ken Cook

TERRY SANFORD, shown above visiting a classroom, was elected Governor of North Carolina in 1960 for the single four-year term permitted by state law. During his campaign and all during his administration he stressed the needs of education, and the results are described in *But What About the People?* In addition to his contributions to education, Governor Sanford established the first state antipoverty program in the country, a local-action program later followed by the Federal Government; reduced the state's prison population by developing a more successful means of prison administration and rehabilitation; and created 100,000 new jobs by bringing in over a billion dollars' worth of new industry and investment—an all-time high. He was the first Southern Governor to call for employment without regard to race, color or creed.

Governor Sanford was born and educated in North Carolina. He lives in Fayetteville with his wife and two children, practices law in Raleigh, and is conducting a study of American states at Duke University under the sponsorship of the Ford Foundation and the Carnegie Corporation.

instruction can mean and he is always ready to give everything. That is why I tell the kids not to be nervous during auditions. The teachers are with them. When artists hear something or watch something happening on stage, the sun opens up for them."

One father, from South Bend, Indiana, who enrolled two young sons in violin and cello, said to us, "This is fantastic. The country's quite excited about your new school. It is amazing that North Carolina would be the pioneer when there are other huge states with enormous wealth that could have undertaken this . . . you might say that yours is the first state legislature to recognize that man does not live by bread alone."

The key to many innovations in North Carolina education has been the use of grants from private foundations. Private money was used exclusively for the Governor's School, and the availability of private matching funds spurred favorable legislative action on the School of the Arts. Compared to the state budget, the amounts are relatively small, but compared to state money available for experimentation, the grants are large and afford considerable flexibility not otherwise possible. The state of Georgia looked at the Governor's School in North Carolina and organized a similar program with state funds. This is the proper sequence. The private money can test out a proposal, a new idea, a fresh approach, and if it appears worthwhile it will be supported by public funds and utilized by other states.

CHAPTER V : The Forgotten Children

Wʜɪʟᴇ ɪ ᴡᴀs ᴄᴀᴍᴘᴀɪɢɴɪɴɢ a lady caught me by the arm at a rally and demanded, "What are you going to do about retarded children?"

It so happened that I had been acquainted for a long time with the work of the North Carolina Association for Mentally Retarded Children, so I had a reasonably ready answer. I told her that every child was entitled to education and training at state expense, and this surely included those with limited abilities. I told her I expected to see that they got their rightful opportunities.

"Well, you'd better," she told me. "They are the forgotten children of North Carolina." Her phrase struck me as stark truth. When I was a schoolboy there was a rather large family living on a farm near town, and the five or six children came every day on the school bus. One was in my class, two were older, and there was a sister or two. But the one I remember most clearly I hardly knew at all. His name was Wilbur. He was roly-poly and had an odd voice. He was mentally retarded.

By sufferance he came to school. There was no place for him but he went to some teacher's classroom; I don't know whose. There were certainly no appropriate books for him and nobody had ever thought of a special training program for him and those like him. He tagged along after a brother or sister at recess. It wasn't unusual to hear a sister screaming, "You leave Wilbur alone!" But his schoolyard tormentors didn't leave him alone, especially when he forgot and was separated from his family protection.

Certainly the school had nothing to offer this child. That it tolerated him must have been some concession, for at that time most schools were maintaining that they had no responsibility for mentally retarded children. Society, maybe, had some responsibility, but not the schools.

The state had a custodial institution even then. But custody is such a small part of the answer—at least nine out of ten of these children are trainable or educable, which means that they will profit by specialized schooling. For years the failure of the state to provide this kind of education placed unreasonable burdens on the parents, who, if fortunate, could at best only band together with other parents and establish, at their own expense, little training groups. This they did in increasing numbers after World War II.

In 1949 some North Carolina schools started their first classes for the educable. In 1957 the first class for trainable children was begun, and North Carolina was not so far behind the nation at that. The first states to authorize classes for these children did so in 1951.

But in the school year 1960–61 in North Carolina only a few more than a thousand trainable retarded were enrolled in special school classes. More than five times that many should have been receiving this training. Fewer than 5,000 of the educable retarded were enrolled out of more than at least six times this number of school age.

There are perhaps four times this many retarded persons in the state, some 140,000. This means that half a million North Carolinians are closely involved with the tragedy of mental retardation, counting parents and brothers and sisters. The effect on the families is often fracturing.

Some of these children, actually a small percentage, will require lifetime care. And yet it has been demonstrated that many of them can absorb training and lead satisfactory and useful lives, given wise guidance and reasonable protection. A limited study developed striking evidence of what might be done to help the educable help themselves. Records of vocational rehabilitation training of 1,500 retarded persons whose yearly earnings before training totaled $70,000, or an average of about $1 per week per person. After training their income jumped to $2.5 million. They became self-supporting and contributing citizens, their days were constructively occupied and far happier, the economy benefited, and the project demonstrated the value of education. We had begun some training in our custodial schools, but not much. In 1960 our vocational rehabilitation programs included only a handful of the mentally retarded.

There were far too many places where the state provided no schooling at all, let alone training in suitable skills. Neither were we doing much to identify retarded children, so that we might start their special education and treatment early. We knew little about mental retardation and were doing so little research. Could it be prevented? What caused it? Scientists amazingly have discovered that the development of at least one type, if identified promptly, can be arrested. What more could be discovered?

Various state agencies were attending to segments of the problem, but responsibility was scattered. And because responsibility was scattered, we had no over-all plan of improvement. I couldn't find any comprehensive recommendations. About all we could do in the 1961 General Assembly was to appropriate all the money requested by the mental hospitals system and blindly add several hundred thousand dollars to the school budget so that we might be in a position to pay any teacher obtained by a local school.

Every agency was anxious to do a better job. We needed some over-all direction of purpose. I had been consulting with leaders of the Association for the Mentally Retarded, and at the time I established a study commission for higher education I decided to fashion a similar commission to study the other edge of our learning needs.

We called it the Governor's Commission to Study the Needs of the Mentally Retarded. The chairman was Charles E. Waddell, a banker and a leader in the association. I also appointed public school people, a pediatrician, a professor of medicine, public health and mental health representation, legislators and other specialists, as well as concerned citizens.

I charged the Commission to "Study the *complete* problems of the retarded child." I asked them to find our failings, to judge the adequacy of existing facilities and programs, to review current research efforts, and to identify and evaluate the needs of retarded persons, from birth to old age.

The Commission's report told us we had shown fairly good intentions for a few years, but hadn't taken enough action. It found very little community understanding of these people and their needs. The Commission concluded that we had not understood enough about the problem to have a unified program. What state agencies were doing, they were doing fairly well with the limited support they had. We were progressing with fragmented programs, and far too slowly.

As a result of this study, in May of 1963 I presented a special message to the General Assembly. I called it "A Proposal on Behalf of the Forgotten Children," and the legislature voted all our requests and endorsed all the specific programs recommended.

Most important, the legislature created the Advisory Council on Mental Retardation. Prior to this no one group had been responsible. Now we had one, a permanent statutory agency which advises and coordinates state agencies in their work with the retarded and studies facilities and needs. It is the official agency to remember the forgotten children, a spokesman and champion for those thousands of citizens who can't speak for themselves. Senator Ralph Scott is chairman of the Council, and it has a full-time, professionally qualified executive director.

The Council consists of representatives of state departments charged with education, public health, mental health, welfare, and juvenile correction. It also includes legislators and private citizens.

The additional appropriations voted by the legislature made it possible for us to say to the local school administrators, "You get a qualified teacher for your retarded children, and we will pay her salary." The State Superintendent of Public Instruction and his staff, especially Felix Barker, Director of Special Education, promoted the program with imagination. As a matter of fact, we provided funds for 661 teachers and ran out of money. Salaries for 892 were requested, far more teachers than anyone thought available. Appropriations for training and education of these children were increased from $865,000 in 1959–61 to over $12 million for 1965–67.

We have not reached all the children, but we have made a start. Over 10,000 retarded children are now able to go to the public schools, like other children, and to be part of their community. They are no longer cut off from the rest of the world because they are different. They can't learn as much as other children, but they can develop to the limits of their own capacities. Our school leaders are making certain that the program expands until special classes are available to the last child.

The Commission also recommended that the legislature start a program of scholarships for teachers who would work with retarded children in the public schools; and we now have ten colleges and universities offering approved courses.

The University of North Carolina, for example, offers 120 state scholarships for summer work, worth $300 each, and eight federal short-term training scholarships. Outstanding teachers who are interested in completing requirements for certification or degree programs in special education are eligible to compete for these scholarships.

Another major educational program is that of operating residential institutions for retarded children and adults who need temporary or permanent custodial care. Until 1957 North Carolina had only one such facility, and it took care of fewer than 2,000 persons. Now we have four, with a total capacity of about 5,500 persons, and a projected expansion to take care of a thousand more. This means that thousands of families are spared the crushing economic and emotional burdens of constant care which some of the retarded require. Moreover, they have the comfort of knowing that the institutions now provide training and rehabilitation; not just custody.

There is a "new look" in these institutions. They are no longer just places where the retarded are sheltered, fed, and forgotten. The Western Carolina Center, for example, which opened two summers ago, was planned to give patients as full a life as possible. The chief architect toured the Scandinavian countries to get ideas on housing for the mentally retarded. Cottage personnel wear cheerful dresses instead of white uniforms. Even the linens and furniture are in such bright colors that one newspaper called the center a "technicolor dream come true." The patients' canteen was developed to substitute for the "corner drugstore" so dear to the heart of teen-agers. Every effort was made to make the physical surroundings and the program as normal as possible.

These "frills," which involve more imagination than money, mean a great deal not only to the students but to the families. Parents suffer a severe emotional jar when they consign their child to an institution, perhaps for life, although it may be the only possible course. The strain is eased when, instead of an impersonal institutional atmosphere, they can see the child in attractive surroundings, with appropriate toys and learning materials, with friendly and trained personnel.

Many retarded persons who are admitted to institutions can be educated to return to their communities. Programs range from religious instruction to job training; from recreation to treatment of physical handicaps; from operation rooms for crippled children to facilities for psychological and psychiatric evaluation and treatment.

Because there is a severe shortage of doctors able to diagnose and treat mental retardation, the state set up a center to train medical students and residents at the University of North Carolina. We also now have the facilities and personnel in the State Board of Health to identify the retarded child and direct him to the appropriate programs. A study made in one North Carolina county, through the cooperative efforts of public and private agencies and interested citizens, revealed that there were about three times as many retarded children in the county as had been known from the records of all agencies. Obviously, you can't do much to help such a child until you learn where he is. Just as we made special classes available in local school districts, diagnostic facilities were made available in the communities, so that parents could learn quickly what was best for their retarded child.

A chief goal was to help older retarded persons to become self-supporting whenever possible. We appropriated enough money to set up vocational rehabilitation programs in all our state institutions for the retarded and similar programs in several communities, and to hire more counselors to work with retarded persons. It has been demonstrated again and again that they can become good workers, and that every dollar invested in vocational training is more than repaid by their earnings. In some routine and undemanding jobs they even do better than the person of average intelligence.

There are many creative approaches to educating and training these people. For example, Reid Ross, school superintendent in my home town of Fayetteville, with the help of such community leaders as Mrs. Mary Pride Clark and Russell Crowell, has converted an abandoned USO building into a workshop and training

facility for mentally and physically handicapped persons. Under
the guidance of Milton Bass, a man of unlimited faith and patience,
students who have finished or dropped out of the special education classes in the schools can learn to earn a living. Some can
graduate to jobs in local businesses; others will remain at the
workshop, which will contract with local firms to do such work
as refinishing furniture and stuffing envelopes for mass mailings.
People who could not hold a job in normal surroundings can earn
money under these "sheltered workshop" conditions.

We need research to tell us what causes mental retardation, and
how we can prevent it; how we can identify those afflicted with
it; and how we can reach into their minds and interest them in
learning the skills and knowledge for which their intellects are
suited. Research has to be a part of each program, so that we can
study what we do, then do it better.

Two of our university medical centers and one of our state
residential centers have under way major research programs in
mental retardation. The Psychology Department of the University of North Carolina is working closely with one residential
center; other parts of our program are integrated with the research effort.

President Kennedy, in calling for federal legislation to help the
retarded, said that "We as a nation have long neglected the mentally ill and the mentally retarded. This neglect must end, if our
nation is to live up to its standards of compassion and dignity and
achieve the maximum use of manpower."

Federal legislation was forthcoming in 1963 to aid and stimulate the development of services for the retarded. But this legislation recognizes, in the words of the President's Panel on Mental
Retardation, that "a successful campaign to combat mental retardation will be staged largely at the state level."

Our program for training and educating the mentally retarded
is many things and many people. It is a specially trained teacher
leading a small child into the world of books. It is medi-

cal students learning to assess the potential of the human mind. It is a teen-ager struggling with a lathe, so that he can later earn a living. It is a skilled and schooled attendant in an institution caring for a person who will never be able to care for himself. It is a sympathetic counselor advising a mother who has been told that her baby's mind will never grow. We have come a long way since the time, only a few years ago, when the only hope offered to the parents of a mentally limited child was that he might, eventually, be admitted to a state institution, where he would spend the rest of his days.

During the summer months after I was nominated I visited all the institutions under the direction of the then Board of Hospitals Control, now the Board of Mental Health. I was accompanied by the board chairman, Representative John Umstead, who is almost solely responsible for leading North Carolina to the fore in the care of the mentally ill. Commissioner Eugene A. Hargrove conducted our tour.

One of these institutions was the Caswell School. As we walked into a room where several children were engaged in a rhythm lesson with drumsticks and other simple instruments, one little boy about seven or eight got up and came over to me. I don't know why. Maybe I reminded him of someone. The teacher seemed a little apprehensive, but she recognized that I was glad to see him and I took his hand. I never did learn his name, but he stood there holding my hand as long as the group remained and talked. Then he said, "Please don't leave me."

"Pardner," I told him, "I've got to go now, but I never will leave you. Do you understand?"

"Yes sir," he told me and released his little grip and waved good-by.

I tried never to leave him. The first annual report of the Council on Mental Retardation summed up the state's efforts by reporting, "These are no longer the forgotten children; they are now North Carolina's 'special children.'"

CHAPTER VI : Education

Beyond the High School

"DEAR GOVERNOR: . . . My father does not earn a very large salary, and there are four other children in my family. I would like to go to Woman's College and my principal thinks I should. I have a B-plus average . . . I have saved some money but not enough . . . I will need financial help. . . ."

During the last two years of my term probably not a single day passed when the Governor's Office did not receive a letter from a student who wanted help in going to college. This was true even in the middle of the school semester, and the number greatly increased in the spring and summer when college decisions were being made.

The reason for this sustained flow of letters was more than the arrival of the much-publicized "baby boom." A far greater percentage of students now are beginning to understand the value of a college education. The estimates are that our North Carolina college population will have more than doubled in the sixties.

The reason the letters were directed to the Governor was a twenty-second radio and television announcement, replayed a number of times, in which I told high school graduates, "If you want to go to college, and you have the will and the skill, but not the money, write to me. Maybe I can help you find a loan."

It was true that there were many loan funds at every college, that the National Defense Education Act provided additional loans, and that many banks had developed college loan plans. Most of these, though, were limited to students who had already entered college. Most were granted to upperclassmen. There were also many "self-help jobs" available at every college, but not enough. Many scholarship programs were provided for the graduate with the better grades.

But it was difficult for a young person just out of high school to get a loan. And if he missed a scholarship, as the majority inevitably did, and if his parents didn't have enough money, he was likely to become completely discouraged. We needed some freshman loans.

We wanted to hold out hope that any ambitious boys or girls, in any high school, could go to college if money was the only thing holding them back. Too many students of ability had not been thinking of themselves as potential college students. We wanted to see them cast themselves, in their minds, in the role of student beyond the high school.

To make this more than a hope we called on the bankers to set up a loan program, available to students in any state or private college, with first priority going to entering freshmen. As a nest egg, and guarantee against loss, we had $80,000 that Luther Hodges "accidentally" picked up while soliciting funds for his Research Triangle, and the bankers made several millions more available. The respective colleges place and administer the loans, but we have an executive secretary to keep it going, and we call it College Foundation, Inc. It is working out very well and will be expanded from year to year. Scholarship programs serve a most useful but limited purpose. The time must come, I think, when ample funds will be available, as loans, for the total college bill of those who need this kind of help.

The student response indicated the demand, and the loan program indicated a part of our concern, but what about the colleges themselves? Could they take care of the demand in adequate fashion? Were they good enough?

Interest in colleges and investment in higher education are nothing new for North Carolina. A few years after the end of the Revolutionary War, amid critical political and economic problems, the infant state established the University of North Carolina. The charter declared that "in all well regulated governments, it is the indispensable duty of every Legislature to consult the happiness of a rising generation, and endeavor to fit them for an honorable discharge of the social duties of life, by paying the strictest attention to their education . . . a University supported by permanent funds and well endowed would have the most direct tendency to answer the above purpose."

A boy walked halfway across the state in 1795 to become the first student to enter the first state university to open its doors. This fact has been a significant influence in North Carolina history. We have been proud of our university and have supported it reasonably well. It is one of the thirty-nine members of the Association of American Universities.

If support and interest are not new, neither is failure in higher education support. Governor Hodges recommended, in the 1961 Budget that he prepared and I presented, $62 million in bonds for construction of college facilities. It was approved by the legislature and submitted to the voters in the fall of 1961. It failed to pass. Some observers blamed this on the reaction to the food tax. I blamed it on not campaigning hard enough.

The best cartoon to come out of the defeat showed a fuming, disgruntled parent leaving a college marked "Sorry! No vacancy," and leading away his son who was wearing a silly grin.

"Tell me again," the boy was saying, "how you showed ol' Terry by beating his bonds back in '61, Pop!"

In any event we just about recovered the loss by the building program of the 1963 legislative session.

Our appreciation of a strong university has continued, even with an occasional setback, but this appreciation is about the only part of the state's position in higher education that hasn't changed. Education beyond the high school no longer means a single university, or a university supplemented by "normal" schools for teachers.

It means, for us, a university with campuses in four cities, concerned with research and public service as well as the education of students. It means senior colleges scattered over the state, whose primary purpose of preparing teachers has been expanded to include general college education in many fields. It means a network of community colleges, technical institutes, and industrial education centers, offering, among other things, college parallel work for two years, training in skills and trades, technician courses, adult education, and retraining programs.

Just as we have been trying to tailor the secondary school system to fit the needs of all students of all abilities and all degrees of aspiration, we are trying to develop a broad spectrum of educational opportunities beyond the high school.

In the first year of my administration, we were certain that a new concept of higher education was needed. Our system was somewhat haphazard, although most of the components were sound. We were not certain what that new concept should be, but we were convinced that the old pattern of the academic college would not suffice; it was not doing the total job. Even better colleges, better supported, would not do the job.

One June day in the mid-fifties, I was at the parsonage of a Methodist preacher who had invited me to make a commencement talk to graduating high school seniors in the town where he preached. It was a class of about thirty, and only six were boys. I didn't wonder where the rest of the boys were, those who had been there as eager first-graders twelve years earlier. I knew.

In the early evening they came to the preacher's house for punch, for trying on caps and gowns, and for the excited conversation common to graduating seniors. The Beatles hadn't come on the scene, so I didn't discuss culture, and had to ask the obvious questions.

"What are you going to do next fall?" I asked the valedictorian.

"I'm going to Queens. I'd like to be a teacher."

Two of the boys were going to college, one to East Carolina and the other to Campbell College.

I asked the class president. "Get married," she said. "He's at State and maybe I'll enroll for some courses."

I asked another girl. "I'd like to get a job in some office. I took typing."

A little bouncy girl with tight pin curls said she wanted to be a nurse and two of her friends and she were hoping to go to the hospital in Fayetteville.

One of the boys said, "I don't know. Maybe I can get a job in Raleigh. A man over in Clinton talked to me about driving a cement truck. I've been driving the school bus, and I might be able to go somewhere if I start with him. One time, a long time ago, I thought I wanted to be an engineer but I don't see much chance of going to college."

One pale little girl said, "I don't know. There's not much of anything to do."

I asked a ruddy, smiling, crew-cut boy, "What are you going to do?"

"What am I going to do? Man, just as soon as I get that ole sheepskin I'm headin' for Carolina Beach!"

He would probably do all right when he got back, too.

But what about the others who didn't see much to do, and the others who had not made it to the senior class? The strength of America, if it depended on education, looked rather anemic that night at the preacher's house.

We had seen the community junior college, partially state supported, grow up in five places. But we knew that two years of traditional college work simply did not match the hopes and possibilities of so many students—we had to offer them more.

We discussed with a number of people their ideas about how to shape a new policy for the state in higher education. We had a nine-member Board of Higher Education, established by Governor Hodges to prevent the overlapping of functions, which served as the clearinghouse for collegiate development, and we thought of charging this Board with working out the new concept for the community or junior colleges. Then, upon reflection, we concluded that a plan involving the community colleges, or even all colleges, would be inadequate. The times seemed to demand more.

Because we needed something better than just more of the same, we evolved the idea of considering education beyond the high school in academic attainment or age. We wanted to consider all needs for education that were not being fulfilled in either the secondary system or the college system. And there were many.

In late summer of our first year we established "The Governor's Commission on Education Beyond the High School." To this commission we appointed representatives of private colleges, of the university, of the state colleges, of the industrial education centers and community colleges, of the legislature, and of the public at large. We charged them with the development of a plan of growth and expansion looking at least twenty years into the future.

This was the "Beyond Commission," as the wags called it, and sometimes it was known as the Governor's Commission, for short, but I called it the Carlyle Commission after its distinguished chairman, Irving S. Carlyle. We set up a staff, headed by John Sanders, later to become director of the university's famed Institute of Government.

It was a working commission, meeting almost every week, studying countless documents, listening to many experts. The members differed and debated with one another, and out of this honest and forceful discussion they hammered out a report that was monumental. It became North Carolina's master plan.

In government, as elsewhere, planning is often a device of delay. If you don't want something done, you set up a planning group. On the other hand, I have also become convinced that not nearly enough planning is done in government. I have been aware of this especially in state government, although I am sure a lack of planning also hampers the growth of municipalities and decreases the efficiency of many federal programs. This lack of standing machinery for planning was illustrated by our need to start at the very beginning in preparing our plan of higher education. We have now designed and established a permanent state planning agency, charged with looking to the future with all agencies and for all programs and activities. A state needs to have plans and projections "at ready" all the time, so the action taken will be as intelligent as possible. Our planning department will bring related agencies together in coordinated planning efforts.

Continuity in state government is easily interrupted and fragmented because the command changes so frequently. This is especially true in a state, such as ours, where a governor may not succeed himself. There are many starts and stops and changes in emphasis. A new governor enters office, greatly interested in some program, which he may promote at the expense of one with which he is less well acquainted, but which is equally important.

It is also true that a Governor loses much valuable action time in drawing together a plan. These plans of action should be kept current, at all times, not only as the basis of action but as the inspiration for new ideas.

I cite this planning program, parenthetically, as a side effect of our college planning effort and to illustrate what needed to be done, and what will be required constantly in the future, if we are to think ahead of all the needs of state government, including education.

In the year I took office I was elected chairman of the Southern Regional Education Board. The SREB had been established by the Southern states, through interstate compact, to help improve higher education through studies and projects, and the pooling of certain facilities for graduate work. A year or so before I took office the SREB, through the inspiration of its director, Dr. Winfred L. Godwin, had commissioned a planning study of higher education in the South. The chairman was Colgate Darden, a former president of the University of Virginia and former Governor of Virginia. Other members were A. Boyd Campbell, Oliver C. Carmichael, Sr., former Florida governor LeRoy Collins, H. H. Dewar, Marion B. Folsom, and Ralph McGill.

It was called "The Commission on Goals for Higher Education in the South." Its purpose is contained in one sentence: "If this region fails to cultivate its intellectual resources, it must abandon hope of directing its own economic destiny." This was the Goals Commission's message to the entire South. That was also the message our administration had been trying to deliver to North Carolina.

In the late fall of 1961 SREB released the Report of the Goals Commission. It was entitled "Within Our Reach," emphasizing that we did have within our reach the strengths to make our resources of higher education the best in the nation.

Without this improvement, I was convinced we could never break out of our role as a "have not" region. Now the Goals report of the Southern Regional Education Board hoisted high the worthy standard. We could see in print what could be accomplished. It was not enough for any institution to say "we are the best in the South," the Commission stated. "We must insist that Southern colleges and universities be measured against the same criteria of excellence which are applied everywhere."

That was the kind of talk I liked to hear. This was a battle standard to which we could all repair. The South will "be economically healthy only if it has the technical training and intellectual development required to exploit the potential of the new science and technology." The South's universities "increasingly must become the initiators, the prime movers of progress. From them must flow the ideas, the imaginative and creative plans, to be translated into action by the people of the South."

This had also been the theme of Howard Odom's monumental study of the Southern regions three decades ago. This was the way for the South to make the most of its human resources. This was the way for North Carolina to stop the human erosion, to protect and develop the talents of her people, to engage in self-improvement through the improvement of education.

Odom had said that excellent opportunities for higher education were a primary need. After listing the usual arguments that the South couldn't afford or didn't need strong universities, he said that "if the nation and the region, after appraising the extraordinary facts pointing to the abundance of natural, cultural, and human resources, still continue in the mature judgment that the region should not and cannot have its first-class universities, then by all inductions and additions the region must remain continuously deficient."

The creation of the Commission on Goals was in itself an acknowledgment that we could no longer afford to do without the best in higher education, regardless of its monetary cost. The institutions of higher education produce our leadership in government, education, industry, and research. They are the source of new ideas and new forces for human advancement.

While this Goals Commission was reporting, North Carolina's Carlyle Commission was working. The SREB report added a note of importance, and indeed urgency, to what our commission was doing, and emphasized again how much the work of our commission could affect the future course of North Carolina.

As we began to search for a stronger structure of higher education, we faced a kind of a collegiate triple threat. The most awesome threat of the three was the gathering, rising, rolling waves of students who could be seen and counted coming up through the school system. Not only were there more students than ever before, but more of them were determined to seek higher education.

Our researchers counted the students and projected the estimated national percentages of those expected to attend college. In the fall of 1960 we had a total of 75,486 students enrolled, 43,758 in state-supported colleges, and 31,728 in private colleges. This enrollment, we were told, would grow to 84,000 in 1963, and by 1970 the students in college would number 157,690. Thus, in a decade, we would have almost twice as many students knocking on the doors of colleges as were enrolled in 1960. Assuming we could provide expanded college opportunities of such excellence as to be worth the effort, the first order of business was to contain the flood tide.

Our predictions were conservative. In 1963 we had 86,085 enrolled, some 2,000 above the predicted high. And where did they come from? The prediction for freshman enrollment was fairly close. The error, the unexpected boom, came from the fact that more students were returning and staying in college than ever before. Thus, the renewed emphasis on higher education was paying unanticipated dividends.

This enrollment, however, was only half of the tide, with an equal increase among those who were competent to pursue education beyond the high school but had no particular inclination to go to a traditional college.

The worst threat to the fulfillment of our expanding college needs, borne on the tide of the rising enrollments, was the costs. We would be required to look at the costs from two points of view. The first one, the state's appropriations, was already stretched thinly across the many demands, including an expanded and enriched secondary system. Somehow we would manage this, although struggling with budgets and limited revenues tends to make you believe in financial contributions from the federal government, where the potential for revenue is much broader than it is for the states. We had to think in terms of additional buildings as well as continuing and spiraling operating costs.

Beyond the public expenditures was the public policy of costs to the students. Many students, otherwise qualified to profit by education beyond the high school, never got up the courage to think about it because getting the money seemed so impossible. If we were going to try to reach everybody, we had to find a way to hold down the costs.

The second threat was that we might allow the standards and faculty competence to drop, or fail to raise them, and we would be taking care of the crowds, but in a most mediocre manner. We would have them all aboard the train, with the whistle blowing, but the train wouldn't be leaving the station.

The Southern Regional Education Board's Goals Report had this to say about the needed quality of higher education: "Southern higher education must seek the highest degree of excellence in whatever it undertakes." It made the important point that "Excellence in an institution is related to its purpose, and it must be measured, in part at least, by how well the institution accomplishes the task it sets for itself. Thus, teachers' colleges, technical colleges, community or junior colleges, liberal arts colleges and universities alike have an equal chance to attain quality."

The third threat was that we might be held back by tradition and the slow-changing forms of college which would miss the needs of too many of our boys and girls. We need classical scholars, and indeed civilization will not make much progress without them. We need engineers, and chemists, and psychologists, and teachers. We needed all these, and more of the same. But in addition we needed a new concept which would make education fit the challenges of our times, changing and configuring it so that all our human resources might be exposed to the possibilities of improvement. If all students are endowed with the intelligence and ability to benefit from college in the traditional sense, and surely they aren't, and if all students, except the seriously limited, require some post-high school education, as surely they will in this moving world, a change in concept is imperative.

One economist points out that "the really serious problem is . . . the need to upgrade whole segments of the population in a very short time." Everything we saw in the future indicated we needed so many more educated people. We needed a new concept in order to reach the large numbers we had been missing, and we needed to reach them with the new kind of education that would be required of them.

To override this triple threat, we charged our Carlyle Commission with developing a total program. They did, and they divided their recommendations into three parts.

The university, at its three campuses, would furnish the graduate studies and continue its established undergraduate responsibilities. The report recommended procedures for expansion to additional campuses, but we would have only one university.

The college system would be increased with three new four-year colleges, and with steps to improve the excellence of all.

A faculty makes a college. Indeed a faculty is the college, and getting professors was not going to be easy. The competition from around the country was severe. College faculty members, long neglected and underpaid and relatively easy to come by, were no longer available on call. They were thoroughly enjoying the long-delayed and well-deserved courtship being paid by colleges far and near. The Southern Regional Education Board reported, as an indication of the rapidly increasing demand, that the region would require an average of 1,305 more Ph.D.'s annually from 1962 to 1970.

We knew we would have to pay higher salaries, not only to compete for those who were available from elsewhere, or who might be enticed away from our campuses, but also to attract more competent people to commit their lives to college teaching.

Paying higher salaries obviously placed an additional strain on the tax revenues, but it had to be done. In the 1961 and 1963 sessions we increased salaries a total of 27 percent. Even so, we have not done enough and unless we do, we will find our colleges, as well as the university, declining in relative quality. Right now we are attempting to set up a number of university faculty salaries in the range of $25,000 to help attract strong faculty leadership to our university campuses.

The purpose of this money and this effort is to achieve a higher degree of excellence, excellence which is so difficult to measure. Our Commission on Education Beyond the High School had this to say about salaries: "If the public institutions of higher education are to have the qualified teachers they must have in order to serve their students, it is clear that faculty salaries, fringe benefits, and other conditions of employment must compare favorably with those of the institutions with which we are competing for teachers." The Commission compared salaries at the university with those of other leading institutions and found them inadequate. It concluded that "we might continue with more extensive analyses of the compensation paid teachers in our public institutions, and most of them would show our institutions at a significant disadvantage in the competition for faculty talent."

Unless we continue to increase faculty salaries we are going to be on the losing side. To use our limited money wisely, to get the most for our investment, we needed to do other things in addition to raising salaries. The Commission laid out a sound policy for the state, and the 1963 legislature translated this policy into achievement.

First of all, we made the University, capstone and heart of any system of higher education, "The" University of North Carolina. Our university, with campuses at Chapel Hill, at Raleigh (established as a land-grant college in 1889) and at Greensboro (Woman's College until 1964) was consolidated under one administrative president in 1931. Needless duplications were eliminated. Each campus has a chancellor.

All this was an excellent start. The 1963 legislature tied these campuses closer together administratively, reserving for the three-part university the responsibility of being "the primary state-supported agency for research in the liberal arts and sciences, pure and applied."

The total statutory definition covered almost every conceivable interest of a university, but of greater significance was the provision that only the university, of the state-supported institutions, might award the doctor's degree. This would be important as we attempted to concentrate our resources for graduate study, having observed in too many states a damaging diffusion of graduate facilities. Limiting doctoral degrees to one university, with three or four campuses, would meet adequately the demand of expanding requirements. It would also give us a concentration for excellence.

A university is so many things that sometimes it is difficult for people to understand. Too many people do not understand that sizable financial support is essential. Historian Allan Nevins points out that the state universities and land-grant colleges were founded as an expression of the democratic idea, and face a continuing fundamental challenge: "How can they equip the rising generation for the free access of talent to appropriate callings and thus maintain an open society?"

No civilization can grow and survive, and no American state can compete and contribute in a meaningful way, without the institution of the academically free university. President Clark Kerr of California's tremendous university, wrote: "The ends are already given—the preservation of the eternal truths, the creation of new knowledge, the improvement of service wherever truth and knowledge of high order may serve the needs of man. The ends are there; the means must be ever improved in a competitive dynamic environment."

Indeed, the ends had not changed over the centuries, but the universities, the means, have. The universities are no longer small, scholarly communities, but are a far-ranging collection of colleges and programs, closely involved in the life of the state and nation.

As late as 1900 the University at Chapel Hill had a student body of about 500. The colleges at Raleigh and Greensboro, which were to become campuses of a consolidated university in 1931, had been in existence just about a decade. The university's total income for educational and administrative purposes amounted to $48,000. As a bit of nostalgia, we are reminded that in 1900 all candidates for the B.A. degree devoted their first year to studying Latin, Greek, English, and mathematics.

In the fall of 1964 the University of North Carolina enrolled approximately 24,700 students at its three campuses in courses ranging from short prose fiction to molecular spectroscopy. It is a vital institution which has shown itself capable of growth along with its parent state, capable of diversification one step ahead of its parent, and all the while without any sacrifice of quality. Instead, the standards of excellence have been constantly raised.

The university includes such elements as Albert Coates' Institute of Government which each year trains in intensive short courses over 7,500 public officials, ranging from constables to city managers. It includes the Institute of Fisheries Research, solving problems of marine life, operating on our coast, more than 100 miles from the closest campus of the university. The Institute for Research in Social Science, the Institute of Outdoor Drama, the extension courses, the "subcampus" at Fort Bragg, the participation in the support of the Learning Institute of North Carolina, are but some examples of the reach and purpose of the university.

Special schools are divided among the campuses, so that there is a reasonable elimination of duplication in graduate or research facilities. For example, engineering is at Raleigh and law and medicine are taught at Chapel Hill.

Disraeli said that "a university should be a place of light, of liberty, and of learning." It must also be a place of leadership. North Carolina's university has attracted industry, developed our mental hospitals, discovered improved products of agriculture, nourished our schools, enriched our lives, and made us money. It is totally involved in the life and civilization of our people, and our purpose in 1963 was to strengthen that involvement.

As the state continues to grow, and as even greater demands are made on the university, additional campuses may be necessary. If they are, such decisions must be made with careful attention to the need and to the available resources. It would be a mistake in judgment and an exercise in vanity for every college to aspire to become a university. A good college is of far more use and influence than a mediocre university, and size has little to do with academic distinction. Certainly adding the name "university" will not make a college resemble a university. We cannot do without our four-year colleges and we cannot afford to have a second-rate university.

The 1963 legislature, in accordance with recommendations by the Commission on Education Beyond the High School, empowered the Board of Trustees of the university to establish new campuses where and when needed, subject to the approval of the Board of Higher Education and the General Assembly. The Boards and the 1965 General Assembly established a fourth campus at Charlotte, our largest city.

This consolidated university approach has worked well for us and will serve us in the future by allowing expansion within a single administrative framework and a single definition of the excellence we seek. It is our deliberately established policy that we should have only one university, and that this university should be supported to the extent that it might rank with the best universities in the world.

It is also entirely true that the university could not have served us nearly so well had it not been for the state-supported colleges spread across North Carolina. While their establishment was sporadic, their results have enriched the lives of many young people and have added to the development of the state.

For one good example, in traveling through the North Carolina counties of the Appalachian west of Asheville you find that the local leaders, the businessmen, the schoolteachers all respond with pride, "I went to Cullowhee." That is the location of Western Carolina College.

North Carolina's Appalachia is not nearly so destitute as the rest of this troubled American region. Among the most redeeming factors has been the presence of Cullowhee, as well as Appalachian State Teachers College at Boone.

The location of these colleges is convincing evidence that the presence of a nearby college attracts students, instills ambition, and leads people to greater personal fulfillment. In turn the people feed the hope of an entire region. To the boys and girls of far western North Carolina, college has not been a faraway place and an unobtainable dream, the stuff of fanciful thoughts as a little girl might consider becoming a princess. College is Cullowhee, is familiar, but once there the student finds dreams he didn't even know existed. There is no way to measure the full significance of this one college, which brought higher education within the sight of thousands of boys and girls.

This is but one of an even dozen examples. We have twelve such colleges. The first to be established, some eighty years after the opening of the university, was a normal school for Negroes at Fayetteville, in 1877, now Fayetteville State College. A few years later an Indian normal school was established, now our Pembroke State College. In 1891 a land-grant college for Negroes was established, the Agricultural and Technical College at Greensboro. In the same year there was established another college for Negroes, Elizabeth City State Teachers College. These early colleges, too, in a period of recriminations and poverty, marked the dawn of promise for the yearnings of the Negro youth. In the next two decades the state acquired or established four more colleges, and in 1923 a liberal arts college for Negroes was established in Durham.

In 1963 three junior colleges, one east, one west, one central, established by local initiative but later subsidized by the state, were converted into state-supported liberal arts colleges and expanded to four-year degree-granting institutions. Broader curriculums have been added at the teachers' colleges, and no longer are students barred from admission to any college because of race. College education, tangible and obtainable, is within the view of every North Carolina boy and girl.

For many reasons, none with any necessary relationship to the level of excellence of the teaching, it is less expensive to attend one of these colleges than the university. It is estimated that it costs a student at least $1,100 a year to attend the university at Raleigh, while the cost of attending one of the twelve state colleges ranges from $613 to $861 including tuition, fees, and room and board (and not including books or travel).

In the fall of 1964 these twelve colleges enrolled more than 25,500 students, some 150 percent more than a decade earlier. While seeking to raise their own quality they were busy gearing up for even greater enrollments.

Everybody should understand, and our college and legislative leaders do understand, that neither the purpose nor the progress of this college system can be measured in the number of students attending them. It is our responsibility to provide for the quantity, but it is our sacred duty to add and enhance the element of quality.

To get this kind of quality, I have become convinced that much depends on the college president. His vision for his college, persistence with governors and legislators, insistence on standards of excellence by his faculty members, inspiration to his students to achieve the best, all combine to determine the quality of his college. I felt that the Governor's responsibility was to support him beyond the call of duty.

In the four years I have had the opportunity to work closely with our college presidents I have felt that it was remarkably possible to measure the college by the man who headed it. If he put undue weight on physical facilities, if he had been reluctant to guide this faculty to loftier goals, if he sought expansion more than excellence, or if students were to him but disciplinary items, you could read clearly his personal shortcomings in the character of his college.

On the other hand, you could just as clearly read his strengths. If the professors stayed in spite of lower pay, if he always wanted more support than he could possibly expect, if he was seeking constantly new vistas of service for his college, if his students were glowing in pride of their college, you knew you had a president worthy of the name. In fact, even if only a portion of these characteristics were observed in the institution, you knew this man was one of the treasures of the state. For such well-rounded leaders are infrequently discovered, and you grow to appreciate these qualities of leadership in almost any degree.

This is the strongest argument for providing more adequate salaries for the heads of our colleges. In 1960–61 the salaries for our college presidents ranged from $10,000 to $14,000, our chancellors were getting $17,000, and the president of the university $20,000, with all receiving residences and some perquisites. In 1964–65 the college president got from $13,000 to $20,000, the university chancellors from $27,000 to $28,500 and the president $30,000. Anyone familiar with colleges will recognize that we are barely reaching the low average.

It is remarkable that we have been able to attract and retain the leadership we have. We need to do better if we are going to compete to become the best.

To tie all these colleges together, with each other and with the university, we have the Board of Higher Education. The director during my four years was William C. Archie, a distinguished educator. It is not a policing organization, although it has statutory authority to grant or withhold permission to begin new courses. It is not a budgetary agency, although it is expected to confer with the Advisory Budget Commission and offer its opinions of priorities when the budget is drafted.

It furnishes statistical services, and limited research facilities. It supplies support for programs as well as budget presentations. For example, its study of faculty pay was instrumental in gaining legislative support for higher salaries. Its studies of library facilities led to broader support of libraries. It is a clearinghouse for ideas. Working with an advisory group of college presidents, including representatives of our private colleges, it is well positioned to formulate the long-range policies for higher education in North Carolina. For example, the Board invited all senior colleges, both public and private, to engage in a cooperative study of teachers' education which was instrumental in developing our new teacher-training programs.

In the past four years I have attempted to follow the public policy of affording support to any college president who had an idea for enriching his curriculum, such as adding a department of music where none existed. I have tried to support higher salaries and faculty recruitment. The budget expenditures for these twelve colleges was $23 million in 1960–61, and we stepped them up to $40.6 million for the year 1964–65. The theory is that a good college is made by getting a good man as president, and then backing him in all his worthwhile endeavors. The theory works.

CHAPTER VII : In-Between Education

W<small>E CAN'T HAVE EDUCATION</small> beyond the high school reach only for those who can reach back halfway. Too many young people of ability have fallen by the wayside because they simply didn't have the basic advantages we so often assume all Americans have. Too many have found college, or any kind of education beyond the high school, out of the realm of the possible, and ability had very little to do with it. We need to provide the advantages, the beckoning appeal, the availability, and indeed, the insistence. We cannot afford to let so much ability escape service to the Nation.

In my college days I worked in a grocery store with a boy who was intelligent, alert, overflowing with pride. As a form of entertainment, he took delight in correcting the grammar of the children of the more affluent families, especially in front of their parents. Somehow, subconsciously, he was trying to demonstrate that his poor home didn't mean he was ignorant.

Clinton, the store manager said, had "a lot on the ball." He made him the chief of the store clerks and the assistant to the assistant manager. He would go on to be a manager in his own right. Nobody had ever given him an intelligence test, but he would have scored high. He was restless. He wanted to move on and show he could do anything. He had finished high school but in his mind college was for "rich kids." There wasn't any other kind of education available beyond the high school.

The war came and he disappeared into the army. I stopped by to see his mother a year ago after hearing he had died in Detroit two days before.

"Clinton hasn't been home in twenty years," she told me. He had been lured, it seemed, to Detroit by some kind of aspiration that didn't quite materialize. He hadn't done well at all.

"His boy was sent to college by his wife's people. He comes to see us every once in a while," she said.

The mother was close to tears. "It's so hard to have to give him up," she said, but in reality he had given up as a failure some twenty years before.

This story doesn't prove anything. One can cite many similar stories, and equally as many with a happier ending. It doesn't prove a thing, but as I was driving away I thought of a contrasting picture of a prosperous and college-trained businessman, who is now a decent and productive citizen in the community. I had a mental image of him as a fat little brat in a grocery store who was saying, "Me and her want some animal crackers."

"You mean," Clint said, "she and I would like some animal crackers."

The advantage of appropriate education had been available to one and not the other. Perhaps additional educational opportunities would have made no difference. I don't know.

It is often difficult to look at the slogans of American education with any depth or precision. It is more difficult for a governor with the responsibility for shaping the character of our schools. As I thought about the meaning of universal education, the truth of our inadequacies grew larger in my mind.

Universal education has been the viable hallmark of democracy, but our education has never been universal. True, we have had some education available almost everywhere, but if universal was to mean what the word implied then we had to break away from the traditional quantitative view of education. We had to make education appropriate and effective everywhere, appropriate to the needs and possibilities of every child and effective for the purpose of society. Each child must have his best chance.

That was the driving force behind the third part of the Carlyle Commission Report—a fresh approach to education between our high school and the college. The community college would be redesigned so it would also reach everybody who didn't want to go to college, who shouldn't go to college, who had already been to college, who had "aged out" without finishing high school, who needed retraining, those in need of technical and specialized training, illiterates, those who wanted college studies but couldn't afford a residence school, and any other groups which time might develop. And this was to be done in such a way that we might adhere to the highest appropriate standards.

The students would be mostly, but not altogether, boys and girls who, ten years earlier, would not have sought any education after finishing high school. In those days you often heard people say "I completed my education at such-and-such high school." No longer can people consider their education "completed." No longer can they consider a high school education sufficient.

Parents everywhere were beginning to grasp the fact that education was not only an inexorable prerequisite for success in today's world but a continuing part of our lives. There would be many high school students requiring education not at all like our conception of college.

How did we know this? One reason we knew it was that educators had been telling us that the high school graduate needed much more preparation in order to qualify for the available jobs. Another reason we knew it was that industries and businesses were seeking and insisting on students with more specialized skills and more intensive training.

Furthermore, we knew it from our own promising experience. In 1957 North Carolina, under Governor Hodges, authorized and began building what we called "Industrial Education Centers." In 1963 the twentieth of these institutions was opened. In 1962 over 20,000 students were enrolled in these centers, some of whom might have gone to a college, but many of whom would have gone nowhere. Here in the classroom was the positive proof of the demand.

I have pointed out that one of the triple threats was that we might be held back by following too closely the traditional pattern of education beyond the high school. I have pointed out that we started our study of all higher education because we were uneasy about the concept of community colleges. Without quite knowing how, we were certain that we needed to redefine and redesign education that was neither collegiate nor secondary. This was to be the most revolutionary development in our system of higher education.

I have already noted that we had been toying with the idea of state-supported junior colleges. We had five but were planning to convert three into four-year colleges. We had twenty industrial education centers, and one technical institute. Already the industrial education centers were teaching government, reading, economics, art, and a score of academic subjects in addition to industrial and business skills. All this provided an excellent beginning, but our problem was to define the needs fully so that we might design adequately the pattern for development.

The community college is a creature of the twentieth century. It began with the establishment of junior colleges, most of them private and church-related, which offered the first two years of college, generally similar to that offered in senior colleges. In 1920 about two hundred of these junior colleges were in operation across the country. By 1960 over 650 junior colleges had been established.

Some of these colleges, it is generally agreed, were not very good, but others demonstrated there was no reason why they should not be of high quality, competent to provide the best instruction. It was our opinion that state-supported community junior colleges could fill a sizable hole in our fabric of higher education, offering many advantages over our traditional approach to college education. For one thing, because dormitories, at a cost of at least $3,000 per resident, and other facilities essential to a residential college are not required, a community junior college is much cheaper to build and maintain. There was also an advantage, many believed, as senior colleges grew larger, in having the more personal atmosphere of a smaller college.

Another and more important advantage was proximity to the students. Again we were reminded that the existence of a college in a community encourages high school students by its very presence. A community college would have the added advantage of being within the financial as well as the physical reach of many additional students.

So, two words kept coming into focus as we looked for a broader mission for the junior college. One was the word "community." We would think in terms of population centers having within a radius of about thirty miles an adequate number of potential students. The other word was "comprehensive." We would attempt to establish the kind of institution that would embrace all the educational needs heretofore neglected, and we would not limit our efforts to the college parallel studies of the traditional junior college.

In a sense the comprehensive community college in North Carolina was the child of the "GI Bill." The sudden influx of returning veterans, eager for education and backed financially by veterans' benefits, led three of the state's cities, Asheville, Wilmington, and Charlotte, to establish community colleges. These were not supported by state aid, but were initiated by local boards of education and financed by tuition payments, mostly from veterans' benefits, and local taxes. As the colleges grew, and as the number of GI students declined, the costs became burdensome for the local tax sources.

In 1957 state aid was commenced and ultimately these were the three colleges organized as four-year state-supported colleges in 1963. In their period of growth and transition they demonstrated the worth of community colleges. Experience had shown that students at these community colleges were serious, studied hard, and were able to transfer and compete successfully in the senior colleges. Experience also demonstrated that these colleges attracted into higher education many students who otherwise would have failed to seek such an opportunity. Subsequently, three additional community colleges were established by legislative action and state aid under the supervision of the Board of Higher Education.

Prior to the establishment of the industrial education centers in 1957, the only industrial education available was that offered to students in some high schools. Governor Luther Hodges was driving hard for new industry and he realized we could not be successful in industrial development unless we had the trained manpower—the technicians, craftsmen, and specialists needed in a modern economy. Dallas Herring, the scholarly chairman of the State Board of Education, who has furnished so much effective educational leadership for North Carolina, accepted the assignment of making the necessary training available. Provisions were made in the law for local communities to erect the approved buildings, and most of the other costs were met through state appropriations and federal funds.

The industrial education centers were operated for adults and selected high school students, and offered specialty programs in technical areas, but not college parallel or junior college studies. They were open to anyone of the required age and competence, and high school graduation was not a prerequisite to admission. A spread of some sixty-five courses was offered.

Our Commission on Education Beyond the High School warned that the community colleges and the industrial education centers would tend to become more alike in the future. The Commission concluded that "the perpetuation of two increasingly similar but separate systems of post-high school institutions of two-year grade cannot be justified either on educational or on economic grounds; and that state-level supervision of the two systems by different agencies will lead to undesirable competition, lack of effectiveness and efficiency, and economic waste."

The community colleges were under the Board of Higher Education, while the industrial education centers were under the local school board and the State Board of Education. They were financed differently. Operating expenses for community colleges came from local taxes and student fees, as well as from state grants which were limited to use for college courses. Operating expenses for the centers were provided by state and federal funds, and no tuition was charged. In the absence of central planning, there was a very real danger that the two types of institutions could develop overlapping programs, with consequent competition for students and danger of waste of our limited finances.

We also had one technical institute operated by a separate board of trustees. Thus, North Carolina's community system of education beyond the high school had developed as a series of three generally parallel programs. In 1963 these three were redefined to form a coherent system.

We had tried the community junior colleges on a limited basis and the industrial education center on a rapidly expanding basis. The single technical institute had been extremely successful. We knew how these would work, what they could do, and whom they would reach. We knew that a true community college should incorporate appropriate technical and vocational work, college parallel studies, and adult education, all responsive to the changing needs of the community being served. We had the framework and the experience to reach this goal, and it could be done rapidly and at relatively low cost.

A Community College System was created and placed under

the direction of the State Board of Education, and we designated the institutions by one of three different names, depending on the scope of its mission. There was the industrial education center already described. We now have only three of these; most have been stepped up to a technical institute. The industrial education centers designated as technical institutes have all the functions of the industrial education center, plus a broader purpose. The distinction is that these institutions also grant an associate degree for the completion of a two-year technical course in various subjects. We now have fifteen technical institutes. Also the industrial education centers and technical institutions have extension units from Murphy on the Tennessee line to Morehead City on the coast.

Then we have the community college, comprehensive in nature, providing all the opportunities of the industrial education center and the technical institute, plus the freshman and sophomore courses of the liberal arts college. We have five of these in operation, and seven more are being built. Others will follow.

Thus, we have three levels of the same thing, with the possibility of all evolving into fully comprehensive community colleges.

To assist in the policy direction of these institutions, the Board of Education appoints an Advisory Council, including representatives of business, industry, and agriculture, and at least two members chosen from the faculties or staffs of institutions of higher education, and two from the members or staff of the Board of Higher Education. The Council gives advice. Policy is set by the State Board of Education. The system has a Director of Community Colleges, appointed by the Board of Education, and our first director is Dr. I. E. Ready who had previously conducted our Curriculum Study.

In addition to this state supervision we have preserved local responsibility in a workable and effective manner. Each institution has a local board, four members appointed by the local Board of Education, and four members appointed by the local County

Commissioners. In the case of the technical institutes and the community colleges, four additional members are appointed by the Governor.

We think this structure will enable the colleges to be operated by and for their communities, with the state providing over-all direction and coordination. This, it seems to us, meets the recommendation of the American Association of Junior Colleges that "The organization, operation, and control of community junior colleges should reflect both a recognition of the institutional integrity of the college and its coordinate relationships with other educational levels within the State."

The greatest danger, which was observed from the beginning of our study, was that we would end up with a poorly staffed, inadequately financed, hodgepodge of colleges springing up across the state, with conflicts between state and local authorities, and many other ills that might beset any new program of this magnitude. We will have our share of growing pains, but we have made a determined effort to identify and avoid all possible problems.

Obviously every community would like to have a college, and just as obviously it would be unwise for us to attempt to support too many, and it would be impossible for us to maintain the standards if the number of them were unlimited. Our law requires a survey to show a genuine need, potential enrollment, availability of adequate financial support, community interest, and unmet needs. It must be demonstrated to the satisfaction of the State Board of Education that neither private nor public colleges offer the educational needs that would be met by the new institution. Furthermore, the local community must vote approval of the necessary local financial support, usually a bond issue and a tax levy. This is a true test of genuine interest.

The present division of financial responsibility requires the community to provide the site and the bulk of the costs of the buildings, and certain other support which amounts to about 15 percent. The state, with what federal support can be obtained from the federal categorical funds, provides the rest.

Student fees have been kept minimal, about $120 for nine months. We have established a student loan fund from private contributions, from which a student might borrow up to $300 per year, which is more than twice the amount of his fees. It is hoped that soon this fund will be large enough to meet the complete need for loans. As in our colleges, we hope to eliminate the lack of finances as a bar to education.

The unique and significant concept is the comprehensive nature of our system. It is a simplification but not an exaggeration to say that these institutions can provide anything educational not provided elsewhere. The President's Commission on Education Beyond the High School pointed out in a 1947 report that "without realizing it we have become a 'society of students.' More than forty million of us—one quarter of the nation—are enrolled in formal education programs. Millions more are involved in less formal educational efforts." Our state recognized this by offering a variety of opportunities for education beyond the high school.

Neither are we unaware of the need for quality, and neither do we intend to allow these colleges to develop as second-rate institutions. Standards of excellence are just as important in training an automobile mechanic as they are in training a physician. It is realistic to recognize that different people have different educational needs, and we are taking precautions to see that no stigma is attached to taking a vocational course instead of a collegiate program.

Neither, I hope, are we going to "certificate and prestige-ize" ourselves out of business. Our mission is the meeting of all the varied needs of all the people, with good and bad academic preparation, with high and low abilities. We will equip the race track for the slow and for the fast.

We have an open-door policy on admissions. Any high school

graduate, or person who is past high school age, through testing and counseling, may be placed in an appropriate program. No one is turned away. Not every person can enroll in a college parallel program, nor even a technical program, but those who lack the essential prerequisites can be placed in a remedial course until they can qualify for advancement. The exit requirements, however, are more stringent than the entrance requirements. The level of achievement must be high enough to meet the standards of the receiving unit, whether it is a college or a job.

We have mobility. An extension unit can be established for a class in one or more subjects in a nearby county, as needed. There is virtually no limit on the industrial and technical courses offered. We tell industrialists we can teach anything. Our courses range from bricklaying to poultry technology to welding to practical nursing.

A 1963 study suggested allocations of programs, drawing on reports of the Employment Security Commission and other sources to estimate the need for new workers in various fields.

It was possible to predict, for example, that the state would need 757 cabinetmakers by June, 1966, not counting those who would be trained by industry, and that 367 of those would be needed in the far western part of the state. While I have some personal misgivings about such precise estimates, I am sure this kind of thorough analysis makes it possible to assure that we are training people generally for jobs that are likely to exist.

We are making many other studies, and while we will not attempt to limit enrollment purely on the basis of such estimates, we do feel a responsibility to be reasonably certain that a student's training will be useful.

Higher education has left the Groves of Academe and come forth into the communities of the state. We are turning out more doctors of philosophy each year, but we are also training more technicians and industrial workers. The student beyond the high school may be an 18-year-old high school graduate. He may also be an adult who finished only the eighth grade and is employed full time, but is finding new opportunities in evening courses.

From the day in 1797 when General William R. Davie, father of our university and hero of the Revolutionary War, wept in the halls of the General Assembly because the members reneged on their commitment to education, the work and tears of many North Carolinians have combined to bring to fruition a program for the second half of the twentieth century. With this system of institutions, ranging from the university to the extension units of the industrial education center, North Carolina is beginning to make universal education beyond the high school a reality.

And as the years pass we must constantly examine our institutions and schools, seeking always those innovations that will enable us to build strength on strength. I am for a system that does not neglect anything or anybody. I say let's challenge young America in every way we can, and build a system dynamic enough to meet the needs of every human being it touches, diverse enough to satisfy the fires of every ambition, viable enough to give outlet to every worthy motivation.

Quantity education is our burden, both because we have more people and because the changing world simply requires education of a far greater percentage of our citizens. We are going to provide education in greater quantitites than ever before. This is not adequate. We must make certain that we also provide quality education, which seeks all people and all hopes and all abilities.

CHAPTER VIII : The Second
Chance

For TWENTY-FIVE YEARS Scott Wiseman was heard over the radio stations across the country, from the National Barn Dance in Chicago. He and his wife were known as "Lula Belle and Scotty." Still relatively young, they have retired to their home in Avery County, in the Blue Ridge Mountains between Spruce Pine and Newland.

Scotty was one of the hundreds of volunteers helping to improve educational opportunities while I was Governor. He served as coordinator of "Operation Second Chance" in three mountain counties, one of the three regions where we tried an experimental approach to the education of dropouts. As warm a human being as any man can be, he made a sensitive appraisal of his mountain school that will help mold the means the whole state might use in reaching the "hard core" dropout.

As a matter of strategy, we had set forth to mount an unrelenting siege on dropouts. First we had been adding variety to the curriculum, providing a broader choice of courses, consolidating schools, and doing numerous other things which we hoped would make the schoolhouse more appealing and meaningful to would-be dropouts. In addition we had an excellent selection of industrial education courses beyond the high school for those who had quit before graduation, but who had the ambition to come back.

In all my school visits I bore down hard on the folly of dropping out. I called the students' attention to a type of boy they probably knew personally. "The boy who gets some kind of job, and quits school, and buys an old car is fooling himself more than he is fooling you. He rides by the school blowing his horn, and with a little change jangling in his pocket, and he thinks he has the jump on you because you have to put up with study halls and homework. But he is not ahead of you and soon he will be far behind you. And he won't be able to catch up or even draw up in sight of you by the time he realizes his tragic mistake. If you finish high school, statistics demonstrate you will earn exactly twice as much in your lifetime as he will during his."

I reminded the boys and girls that North Carolina and the United States needed them all. "North Carolina cannot spare a single trained mind. When you let yourself remain weak you make your state and nation weaker. We can't do without you. Not a person in this room would be known as a draft dodger in time of war. North Carolinians have always answered the call to duty when our land and freedom were imperiled. Today your nation needs not your strong back to carry a rifle. It needs your strong minds and educated brains. If you don't finish school you are not doing your duty. If you drop out of school it is the same as hiding in the hills of Tennessee in time of war to escape the draft."

In addition, we had state committees, local committees, and a well-designed effort to eliminate some of the other causes or excuses for leaving school before graduation. When we haven't done a good job of teaching reading in the lower grades, the curriculum gets pretty incomprehensible by junior high school. State Superintendent Charles F. Carroll had recognized this and

drew up plans to correct the deficiency. There are other academic inadequacies which increase the traffic to the exits. It is
also quite true that the lack of decent clothes has embarrassed
many girls and boys out of school, quite unnecessarily of course.
And it is a fact that high fees for extras have made quitting easier.
The lack of encouragement from parents who simply do not
understand the importance of schooling takes its toll. Many
parents who do appreciate the value of school cannot, for various
reasons, communicate this urgency to their teen-agers. Dropouts,
it is obvious, fit into no single mold.

It wasn't that our dropout rate was getting worse. It was
improving considerably. At the same time, however, any dropout
rate became less tolerable. As Secretary of Labor Willard Wirtz
told a conference of the National Committee for Support of the
Public Schools, "The dropout problem is not that there are more
dropping out. The problem is that there is a much smaller
demand for unskilled workers in the work force than there was
before. . . . We no longer have the absorptive quality in the
work force to take care of the mistakes we made in the educational system."

We were finding that fewer were dropping out, and more
were coming back for additional schooling in the industrial
education sections of the community college system. We had
many young people, however, who for various reasons lacked the
self-generating ambition which would lead them back to the
classroom. Maybe they didn't know where to go or how to
apply. Maybe they didn't know that there was a second chance
available for them. Maybe they had lost all self-confidence.

We had to pick up these fragments of our past mistakes, no
matter how effective our programs for the future might prove.
We had to find a way to get to those who wouldn't come on
their own initiative. Otherwise we would forever have them with
us, progressively becoming a heavier burden for society to carry.

We wanted to be able to go out and find them, and say to

them, "We have set up a new kind of special school so you can come back and have a second chance." If we didn't do this before they were totally beyond recall, we would miss all chance to redeem them.

The federal government had set up a program of retraining for unemployed workers. To be eligible one had to be unemployed, and meet certain other conditions. Those who took training were paid about the equivalent of unemployment insurance for the duration of the training. The state school system and the employment security offices cooperated in this plan all over the state.

The only serious difficulties we encountered were delays in the required procedure of approval. Frequently these delays caused us to lose some of our prospects, but otherwise this kind of training worked out fairly well.

It seemed to us, however, that the eligibility requirements eliminated the young people who most needed the training, and that it would be much better if we could enlist them before they aged into eligibility. George Stephens, Jr., my assistant for economic development, and Gerald James, the supervisor of vocational education in the State Department of Public Instruction, worked up some ideas. The staff of the U.S. Department of Labor responded with enthusiasm and designed an experimental project.

We signed a contract with Secretary Wirtz for three special schools to be known as "Operation Second Chance." Funded by the Office of Manpower, Automation and Training, as well as Area Development Administration, the schools would provide vocational and academic education for those who had not finished high school, and were between the ages of seventeen and twenty-one. They would be run by our industrial education centers. In Lincoln County, in the center of the state, the classes were held at a vacated school. In the mountains we acquired the use of abandoned school buildings at Spruce Pine and Burnsville, but the administration was handled from our Asheville Industrial Education Center. The third school was in Eastern North Carolina at Columbia. The students were given placement and aptitude tests and counseled as to their capabilities and interests. They were paid $24 a week.

When I stopped by our Spruce Pine School I found a half dozen boys almost inside the engine of an old Chevrolet. They were beginning to learn a trade for the first time, and today most of them are employed as automobile mechanics.

Quite a few girls were working in upholstering, getting ready for jobs in the nearby furniture industry. Others, taking a break from their training in skills, were upstairs under the helpful eye of a teacher as they pored over their self-teaching books in an English class.

I talked to one lad who was holding his welding torch, his eyeguard pushed back to view the line weld he had formed. "How much school have you had?" I asked him.

"Well, I got to the eighth, but I didn't finish it."

"Do you think you can be a welder?" I asked.

"I sure do, and when I finish I can get a job. There's a shortage of welders."

I reminded him, "You'll have to go somewhere else to get a job, I'm afraid."

"Yes, I know it. But that suits me fine."

I asked about his academic studies, and he told me about his reading. It had been so painful when he was in school before. "And you know, Governor, this is the first time fractions has ever made any sense to me."

Not much of a commentary, maybe. But I was glad they made sense, and doubtless in his new job in his new place he would be able to put them to good use. In any event his enthusiasm for learning, for the first time in his life, was unmistakable.

Norman M. Chansky, School of Education, North Carolina State University, has prepared an exhaustive and scientific report of "Operation Second Chance." Entitled "Untapped Good: The

Rehabilitation of High School Dropouts," it is easily among the best works in the country, and should be studied carefully by all who would recruit dropouts for further training. "Operation Second Chance" was not organized as a permanent program; rather it was a demonstration project designed to guide us to better methods in our industrial education centers and other schools. The Chansky analysis makes possible the expansion of what we have learned to the entire system of education.

I also got a verbal summary from Scotty Wiseman: "It has done a lot of good, but I think we could do better. I noticed that they began to dress a little better, and to take care in their appearance. You forget that their experiences up to that point haven't done much to build their pride. Generally their home background has not been good. They haven't had any encouragement. They haven't believed they could do anything. Nobody has pushed them. They don't have much of an outlook.

"I wish the program wasn't running out. I would like to see us do some other things. For one thing I think we should give them a physical and help them get straightened out where possible. Almost all of them need work on their teeth. Many of them need glasses. They haven't had proper nourishment, and it shows. They don't know how to get these things for themselves, and they need somebody to show them. This might not be education, but it surely would help their education.

"It's mighty easy to just say they are worthless and throw up your hands and walk away. They never had learned good work habits and promptness. Some of them would begin to shape up. Everybody has some goodness inside, and it just has to find a way to come out. I suppose they might not have been dropouts in the first place if they had had somebody to teach them good habits of living and work."

I wanted to know if he thought the program was successful.

"Yes, generally. We had 475 originally lined up, but it took too long to get the courses approved and too many of them drifted away. We trained 179 and I would say we were about 65 percent successful in getting them placed in jobs. I had said if we did some good for 10 percent it would be worth the effort. So it was successful. Some wouldn't leave home to take jobs. I think they were afraid to leave their mountains, so maybe we left something out of their education. Maybe they just don't feel they can deal with the city life, but they might if we could guide them a little more. I can't really blame anybody for not wanting to leave our mountains, you know. That's why all of us are working to get more industry in here.

"I was disappointed in what we could do for the girls. I wanted to get some training courses for catering to the tourist trade, but we couldn't get this cleared. It seemed to me we had too many rules and too much red tape. I don't know. I don't want to criticize, because everybody tried to make it work. Sometimes rules get to be more important than the people we are working with, and then we are missing the point."

I asked him how he got the students to enroll. "How do you go about signing up your students? How do you get their interest?"

"We had stories in the papers and announcements on the radio. We talked to clubs and churches and individuals and asked them to help us find young people who needed this training. The schools were very helpful in telling us about prospects. I stopped at stores and filling stations to try to find those out of school and unemployed. Then we went into the coves and hollows to find them. You had to sit on the porch and rock. You had to talk their language."

The one lesson all of us drew, from all the schools, was that recruiting was essential. In time we can develop better recruiting techniques, but we must have recruiting. This kind of prospective student is not likely to be a newspaper reader. He is not likely to respond to a radio spot. It is necessary to seek him out, to sell him on his own worth, to give him the encouragement he lacks. It is necessary to have recruiters who do "speak their language."

In some instances it is a matter of merely letting them know that the opportunity exists, that at a certain address there is an open door with tools inside that fit his hands and instructors who will teach him. A shocking number of society's stepchildren, as they have been called, are generally ignorant of many of our programs, including the industrial education centers. Their plight is compounded by the sense of estrangement that is natural to one who has cut loose from his moorings.

The official final records of the total project indicate that we enrolled about twice as many as completed training, and that most of these got jobs related to their training. It was a worthwhile experiment because it demonstrated that these bedrock dropouts can be reached, and can be trained, and can find useful work.

It is not fair to expect any experiment to be totally successful. Dr. Salk used many test tubes before discovering his polio vaccine. We missed many dropouts we should have reached. But we discovered and reclaimed many we had been missing and losing by traditional methods.

I would like to see us put these discoveries to good use. That was the purpose of carrying on the experiment. I would like to see us have a recruiting staff in every industrial education center. I would like to see us call on volunteers in every community to help us seek out those who have been lost to learning, providing for them sympathetic encouragement and guidance to which we have demonstrated they will respond.

If a child misses the first chance presented him by the school system, he is entitled to a second chance. And if he misses that, he is entitled to a third chance. We need a system that is not content to let a single one get away.

Many of the troubles of juvenile delinquency, and much of the population of our prisons, can be traced to inadequate education. It is far better for all of us if we can provide this kind of second chance before ignorance and lack of learning capacity lead to this kind of criminal involvement.

If we haven't provided it, and if this lack of training has contributed to imprisonment, it is still not too late to provide the second chance. In fact in many ways a prison provides an ideal climate for education. At least we "have their attention" and do not have to go out recruiting them.

Our correctional institutions, like most correctional institutions for juveniles, put much emphasis on education. In fact they are just schools, with a few other responsibilities added because of the special circumstances. Their main purpose is education. Ours have been fairly successful. The records to date show that 94 percent of those who attend never get into criminal trouble again.

On the other hand, the prison system has not always been regarded as an educational institution. It should be. It can be most effective.

George Randall, North Carolina's Director of Prisons since 1960, is an unusual man. A textile executive, trained in the law, experienced in the legislature, he chose a public service career out of a deep sense of dedication. He has changed the thinking of veteran guards and prison employees. No longer are our prisons merely places of retribution. They are places of rehabilitation. We now have, and for several years have had, a decreasing prison population, contrary to national trends. Fewer and fewer are coming back.

Rehabilitation is more than formal education. It is, first of all, an attitude—an attitude that must find expression in every employee and official of the prison system. It is our "work release" program, which places over 10 percent of the inmates in work at regular outside jobs, "rooming and boarding" at the prison and paying for their keep, contributing funds to the support of their families, and saving funds toward their release. It is an Alcoholics Anonymous program in every camp. It is a prison industries plan which assigns useful and profitable jobs to every able-bodied inmate. Finally, it is education.

Any inmate who comes into the prison unable to read and

write, and who is not retarded, must go to school. In addition, there is a broad variety of education available for those who need their second chance at schooling. In the spring of 1964 the prison system graduated its first class at our industrial school, established at an old prison camp. Here young men have an extensive choice of vocational training.

Another heartening example of the prison educational program is that of the women's prison. Out of about 400 inmates, some 250 are enrolled in classes. The prison has four full-time teachers, one part-time, and one principal. Many of these women prisoners are illiterate when they arrive. Even the rudimentary skill of learning to sign one's name is a substantial step toward correcting the maladjustments that led to prison.

We also set up prison high schools. We have, as do most other states, a high school equivalency test. This is administered by the State Department of Public Instruction, and those who do the necessary work may earn a certificate. It is equivalent to a regular diploma for all practical purposes. The availablity of this alternative made the prison high school feasible.

Through study in regular classes 15 inmates of the Correctional Center for Women in 1963 earned their high school equivalency diplomas. The number grew to 22 in 1964. My wife made the first commencement address, at the regular graduation ceremonies, and the graduates wore caps and gowns.

Afterwards there was a reception for the graduates, who had been allowed to invite their friends and families to the exercises. The impact of earning a diploma on these women who had failed in so many ways is hard to imagine. It is perhaps illustrated best by the fact that even those who had been released before graduation returned to prison to take part in the ceremonies. They have finally "made good" at something, and they are rightfully proud. One girl returned by bus all the way from New York to participate in her graduation day.

One of the inmates made and presented to Mrs. Sanford a

ceramic statuette, a figure of a graduate in cap and gown, with the initials W.C.C.H.S.—The Women's Correctional Center High School. It stands in our home on a shelf along with Terry Jr.'s trophy for midget football.

Such are the results of second chances. I am not hard-boiled enough to agree that this amounts to "coddling" prisoners.

CHAPTER IX : The Cycle of Poverty

"THIS IS MY BRIARPATCH," says John H. McInnis, 46-year-old principal of Ashley Chapel School. Here he has worked for years in a place called Mizpah, where the sandhills run into the red clay of the Pee Dee. It is an unusually impoverished Negro settlement where the soil is so weak that most of the residents do not even try to have gardens. The prospects for farming are so poor, they will tell you, that "you have to stand knee-deep in a sack of fertilizer to raise your voice."

The Mizpah Improvement Association wants to raise not voices but the income of the community residents. There are jobs in nearby Rockingham, if you have a skill. There is a new Technical Institute between Hamlet and Rockingham where vocational skills are taught. But a person without the ability to read and write will find it difficult to enter, and impossible to keep up. And many of the Mizpah residents are illiterate. McInnis sent his teachers out to find these people, then set up special classes to teach them to read and to show them the way to the Technical Institute.

All this is a small part of a project called Tri-County Community Action, which, along with ten other generally similar community projects, sprang from the sponsorship of a new organization named The North Carolina Fund.

The Fund was started because we were looking for ways to help the children of blighted places like Mizpah. And now, as it turned out, the parents were involved in schooling, too. Mizpah discovered that the parents had to be helped in order to help the children.

I was invited to give the Alfred D. Simpson lecture at Harvard University, and I decided to talk about some of these children.

"I remember a little girl, with golden blond hair, in the second grade of a school in the Great Smoky Mountains of my State," I told them. "She couldn't read . . . the teacher said she didn't fit in and didn't like school."

I tried to talk with her but she simply looked at the floor. She was shy and silent and seemed unhappy, and apart from the fun of school. In time we learned more about her, and others like her.

I told the audience, "These are the disadvantaged children. And this is the largest and the most difficult of all the groups in our schools needing our special attention."

An exaggeration? Hardly!

There actually was such a little girl. Her name is Mellisa. John Ehle had pointed her out to me on one of our school visits. After I talked to her I asked John to find a casual way to call on her parents, to look at her home, to find out what he could. We wanted to discover some of the reasons why she, and other little children like her, found school so hard to "fit in."

Was it the school? Or were there other reasons?

It was apparent that she was not mentally retarded. She was a lovable little girl, and probably bright, so what was it?

Her family, John reported, had come from the sturdy pioneering people who had settled the Appalachians. As she grew to school age she had watched her grandfather hitch the mule to the plow, had seen him use the anvil and hammer and chisel to fix the chain for the singletree; she had helped her mother milk the cow. Mellisa would sing too, songs some happy and some sad, that had been sung in those hills at least since the days of Daniel Boone.

Hers was a wonderful world, but the times were passing it by. Hers was a nonverbal world, although of course she didn't know this and wouldn't have known what it meant. Neither would her parents. They worked hard. They were respectable and decent, and every Sunday morning they went together to a little dingy white frame church. But they couldn't read. They didn't have any books. They were not acquainted with newspapers, except as something provisions from the store were sometimes wrapped in.

Why couldn't she fit in at school? "Isn't there some way that school could be more receptive? Couldn't it bend to her needs?" Ehle asked.

Could we not find a way to shape her native ability and experiences into motivation, understanding, and achievement? Couldn't her love of music and songs be used to help her grasp words and books and the meaning of reading and learning? Couldn't we use educational toys, puzzles, and other unconventional techniques to show her the way of study? Why couldn't we build on what she had learned at home to make school a happy place where new wonders were sought and discovered?

Robert Hummerstone, staff writer for the Charlotte *Observer*, described another little girl, "in the first grade at Charlotte's Villa Heights School, who has never been to the airport, or seen a movie, or seen the ocean. She's not even sure whether to eat her free school lunch with a fork, a spoon or her hands. . . . She's already lagging behind her classmates only two months after school began. . . . She's never known her 'Daddy.' And mother has left her with another family to look for work. . . . There are no books or magazines where she lives, so when she got her first schoolbook she didn't know which was its front, which its back."

Mellisa was so much more fortunate than the Honey Randolphs and the Villa Heights child. There was nothing sordid about her home life. But all three of these children were of the same genus, the disadvantaged, from homes where the lexical skills were unknown or disdained, where there was little preparation for what school would later require of them.

The disadvantages were varied and many, but all of the disadvantages led to one common difficulty. These children came into a school system not organized to treat with them. They came and found school a strange world they had never known. They had no idea of how in the world you might get something useful from a piece of paper with little marks on it. And they had no idea why you should *want* to get anything good from such a marked-up piece of paper.

Later we were to find whole neighborhoods of children who had never even heard a nursery rhyme. They didn't know Cinderella and had never sung about the mulberry bush. They came to school without the advantage of knowing how to shape their names, without the advantage of being able to count even a few numbers. They came without knowing their ABC's, and as often as not, without knowing there were any ABC's.

They might be Negro, white, or Indian, living on the farmland of the coastal plains, or the mountains, or in the crowded housing areas of the Piedmont, the children of decent people, or irresponsible people, or criminal people. They were everywhere and anywhere. They were caught in a cycle of poverty, condemned to remain in poverty, and destined to raise their children in poverty.

I think I was justified in saying to the Harvard audience, "These are the disadvantaged children, and this is the largest and most difficult group needing our special attention."

How to go about it? Improvement of schools wasn't enough. Not nearly enough. If school was to have any meaning for them, these children first had to be put in a position to understand why learning was important, to comprehend what school was all about. This was the only way they could break out of the cycle of poverty in which they were entrapped.

The place to start, it seemed to us, was in the first grade and even before that.

One evening Charles Babcock, Anne Reynolds Forsyth, and several others were sitting at the Governor's Mansion discussing a number of things, including a project in remedial reading which had been sponsored by the Mary Reynolds Babcock Foundation.

In a public school with which they were working in Winston-Salem, it had been discovered that about 50 percent of those finishing the third grade were not able to read and write acceptably. This inadequacy applied to children of all races, although the disadvantaged, including the Negroes, were most likely to be those who fell behind. The Babcock Foundation project identified these slow ones, provided remedial reading opportunities, and by the sixth grade most of them happily had caught up.

"Why," it was asked, "cannot we do the job right the first time? Then we wouldn't need the remedy treatment."

This made sense to me. Convinced that we were failing to teach well enough in the first grades, I had long made an offhand hobby of asking first-grade teachers what they most needed to improve teaching. "Fewer students" was the inevitable and unanimous reply.

"How much," I sent a memorandum to the Comptroller of the Board of Education, "would it cost to double the number of first-grade teachers?"

"$7,532,840.28" was the reply. "But the chairman reminds me that even if you find the money we can't find the teachers." So what could we do? We could experiment.

Everett Miller, a man who is not afraid of a new idea, North Carolina's Assistant Superintendent of Public Instruction, had been studying with his associates the possibilities of experimenting with better organization for the first three grades, and they came up with some good ideas.

He prepared a proposal for a national foundation—Ford, he hoped—to demonstrate that the quality of teaching could be improved in the first three grades. He wanted to try preschool readiness classes, teacher aides, team teaching, ungraded classes, and any other good idea which might be suggested. We were convinced that the answer for the disadvantaged was a new dimension for education not yet fully implanted anywhere.

Many other suggestions came to us, including neighborhood, health, rehabilitation, and employment programs, all aimed at removing some of the disadvantages that burdened these children. Ultimately we had numerous ideas, concepts, doubts, and approaches floating around the Capitol. Now we needed precipitation to get them down to earth.

John Ehle had been talking to Paul Ylvisaker of the Ford Foundation. Ylvisaker had sparked the gray areas programs across the nation; at Boston, New Haven, Oakland, and Washington. These projects, in turn, would later spark the national Economic Opportunity Act. These were the early skirmishes in the war on poverty.

However, we were not plagued with the gray areas problem in the same sense as were these selected cities. Furthermore, I was not essentially interested in a single community—our duty was to the whole state. Also, I had begun to realize that I had stumbled into the whole confusing pattern of poverty in America while trying to find better ways to educate the children of the disadvantaged.

Joel Fleishman, John Ehle, and I went to New York to call on the president of the Ford Foundation, Henry Heald. With him were Clarence Faust and Paul Ylvisaker.

"I didn't come here to get any money," I told Dr. Heald. "I'm not sure we want any money. We don't have a proposal to present. We do want your advice and the benefit of your experience."

Probably this was a somewhat unusual experience for foundation officials. But it was not a designed approach. It was an honest expression of doubt.

"You are concerned with disadvantaged areas, and we too are determined to try to do more for the education of our disadvantaged children. We want to lift the children out of the conditions of poverty and help them become self-supporting. We would like to see if we might accomplish something across an entire state."

I requested that Ford send down a group of its staff to visit around the state with us, and to seek the answers, and to tell us what they thought we might be able to do.

"After that, if we see how it can be spent beneficially, we might ask for a grant. And we might not."

They came. Clarence Faust, Paul Ylvisaker, and a half dozen others. We flew them in the *Kitty Hawk,* the state's small airplane, and another plane pressed into service, from the Appalachian counties of Watauga and Avery to Winston-Salem, to Charlotte, and down east to Greenville for conferences with countless people.

They then came to the Governor's Mansion to recuperate.

The idea of state action to break this cycle of poverty was beginning to take shape. It would be a matter of specialized education. We would have to do some experimenting to design it.

We visited the special schools in New Haven. Members of the Department of Public Instruction looked closely at the project in Oakland, California. We held conferences and extracted advice from people all around the nation.

We wanted an answer to the question: How do you use education to destroy the forces that condemn so many children to lives of poverty?

We concluded that it could be done, and that the burden should be carried by local leadership. We thought the role of the state was to make its service agencies more efficient and to encourage local leadership.

On the basis of the conclusions we incorporated, on July 17, 1963, a private and nonprofit organization, "The North Carolina Fund." One of the incorporators was Charles Babcock, along with several who were later to be selected as members of the Board of Trustees.

This approach was taken, rather than the establishment of a state agency, because we would need the flexibility to gather in private funds and to experiment with the greatest possible degree of freedom.

The Charter provided authority to study the educational problems, economic opportunities, living environment, and general welfare of North Carolinians; to make grants for research and pilot projects; to furnish staff services to public and private agencies; to encourage cooperative state and community action.

Charles Babcock took us to see Mrs. Nancy Reynolds Verney, and we made a transatlantic call to Richard J. Reynolds, Jr. We asked for their help and got their enthusiastic support. The Z. Smith Reynolds Foundation and the Mary Reynolds Babcock Foundation would help match any funds we might obtain from Ford.

On August 12 we presented a formal proposal to the Ford Foundation. We told them, "We want to concentrate on experimental action programs . . . to encourage comprehensive community projects . . . to encourage experimental projects by State agencies . . . to encourage local governments and community agencies to re-examine critically what they are doing and determine how new ideas and new approaches can produce better results. . . .

"The North Carolina Fund asks that The Ford Foundation join in this new and unprecedented state enterprise by making a grant of $7,000,000. . . . That of this initial grant $2,000,000 will be applied toward the proposal of the State Board of Education for a major school improvement project in the first three grades of school."

Ford made the grant of $7 million, which was announced in September, 1963. Reynolds granted $1,625,000 and Babcock $875,000, and with matching community support we had available some $14 million for five years of experimental action.

For our executive director we drafted George H. Esser, Jr., professor of Public Law and Government and assistant director of the Institute of Government at the University of North Carolina at Chapel Hill.

We gathered a representative Board of Trustees: Hargrove Bowles, Greensboro businessman and chairman of the State Board of Conservation and Development; Gerald Cowan, Asheville banker and former member of the State Board of Education; Dr. Samuel E. Duncan, president of Livingstone College and a member of the State Board of Welfare; Dr. Hollis Edens, former president of Duke University and executive director of the Mary Reynolds Babcock Foundation; Mrs. H. Frank Forsyth, Winston-Salem leader and a board member of the Z. Smith Reynolds Foundation; James A. Gray, president of Old Salem, Inc.; Dallas Herring, chairman of the State Board of Education; Wallace Murchison, Wilmington attorney and leader in court reform; Mrs. B. C. Parker, a long-time member of the Board of Trustees of the University of North Carolina and a retired public school principal; and former House Speaker, and leading university trustee, Thomas J. Pearsall. C. A. McKnight, editor of the Charlotte *Observer*, was made president, John H. Wheeler, banker and a member of the President's Committee on Equal Employment Opportunities, was chosen as treasurer, and I was elected chairman of the Board. One vacancy was later filled by Mrs. Dan K. Moore, wife of the present Governor.

"The idea for The Fund originated," Billy E. Barnes, news director for The North Carolina Fund wrote, "when Governor Sanford, having spent two years of his administration building a better school system in North Carolina, came to the realization that improved education doesn't necessarily improve, significantly, the plight of the poverty-level child. Why? Because these children have so many distractions—hunger, sickness, crowded living, and poor studying conditions—coming between them and their lessons that they can't take advantage of what the school has to offer."

Barnes was right, except that the Fund idea originated when *many* people in state government began to realize that we had to make education reach further than it had been reaching.

We intended always that the Fund should be an educational organization. True, we were describing an unusual and unorthodox kind of education, but nonetheless education. That the Fund was to strike at the cause of poverty in many ways is simply a manifestation of our belief that the children of poverty need special breaks if they are to be able to compete in our school system. It is also an expression of belief that education is the best instrument for breaking the cycle of poverty.

The Honey Randolphs, the children caught in the cycle of poverty, have found little success in our public schools. It is not a valid explanation to attribute their failures to stupidity, or ineptness, or inherent slothfulness. There are too many of them. I agree with Michael Harrington that "the real explanation of why the poor are where they are is that they made the mistake of being born to the wrong parents. . . . Once that mistake has been made they could have been paragons of will and morality, but most of them would never even have had a chance to get out."

We could not very well continue to overlook these children when we had declared a policy of educating all children, wherever they might live, whoever their parents, no matter how much money they might have, regardless of their color, and whatever their limitations.

In North Carolina, according to Michael Brooks, staff member of The North Carolina Fund, in his *Dimensions of Poverty in North Carolina*, 37 percent of all families had incomes of less than

$3,000, and 11 percent had family incomes of less than $1,000. This doesn't mean, in my view, that all these people are living in poverty.

Poverty means more than being poor. Brooks put it this way: "The culture of poverty is characterized by disadvantage, deprivation, and disability. Its members are those persons who lack education and skill, and are thus faced with unsteady employment and low incomes. They live in slums, both urban and rural; their housing is dilapidated and overcrowded. Their physical health is poor, and the stresses they undergo in their daily struggle for existence result in high rates of mental illness. They are, in short, 'multi-problem' families and individuals, caught in a web of interwoven disabilities."

This is the physical view. Brooks also talks of the poverty of the spirit. "The impoverished view the world as a hostile environment, offering no opportunity for self-improvement. It is true that many of those living in poverty lack aspirations and initiative—but only because of the utter futility of aspiring for things which seem impossible to attain."

In reality, it is not poverty we have set out to fight. It is the *causes* of poverty. Much as we would like to, we cannot identify poverty and erase it. Providing jobs, increasing minimum wages for unskilled labor, providing additional artificial earnings by whatever device, is at best no more than an alleviation and temporary cure.

We cannot even rescue everybody caught up in poverty. That is unfortunate, but to suggest otherwise is to delude ourselves, and if our objective is ill-defined, we risk total failure.

We can, perhaps, use education as the lifeline for rescuing those who are young and resilient enough to participate in their own rescue. And in the process of rescuing the young we may succeed in breaking the cycle of poverty.

In announcing our assault on the causes of poverty, and the establishment of The North Carolina Fund, I expressed our concept in this way: "I have come to believe that charity and relief are not the best answers to human suffering, that the schools are not the answer so long as only half of our students finish school, that the wealth of America is not the answer if many families have fifty-some cents a day per person for all expenses; that it is not enough to have here the most powerful nation in the world and then to admit that we are powerless to find ways to give all of our young people training and job opportunities."

In North Carolina we wanted to say to the community leaders: Let's see if we can show how education, combined with welfare, health, employment, and other public and private services, can be used to stop wasting lives and burdening American society with a handicap it need not carry.

We hoped our experimental programs in a few selected communities would lead to success, and that our successes could later be translated into widespread improvement of our schools, agencies, and institutions.

Two guides were prepared.

One, drawn up by The North Carolina Fund, described how community leaders might go about planning a comprehensive community action program. We invited them to get together and to see how they might discover the poverty in their own neighborhoods, and how they might do something about eliminating the causes of poverty. We promised we would help finance the eight or ten best projects, but we were convinced that even if a community didn't get finances from the Fund, ideas would be developed and action taken.

We had anticipated receiving some twenty proposals, hoping they would come from all parts of the state, so that we might have for our experiments the choice of representative counties and communities.

On our deadline, the first week in February, we received over fifty proposals, covering sixty-six of our one hundred counties.

Our small staff advised on methods, but the ideas had come from the local leaders. Some of the ideas for needs and methods had come directly from those who were caught up in the claws of poverty.

Our Board members formed teams with our staff members, and visited every community that had submitted a proposal. This was perhaps the most thorough tour of poverty areas undertaken in any state. We confirmed the need in every spot across the state.

We also confirmed our confidence in the initiative, originality and concern of our local community leaders.

The proposals were generally comprehensive, with most of them suggesting from three to fifteen different activities. It is impossible to list all the ideas that were offered, but Craven County, for example, as one of its several projects, suggested a preschool readiness program that would include day care services for children of working mothers. Guilford County made a similar request to expand an existing program and to establish new facilities. Duplin, Wayne, and Greene Counties proposed as one of their approaches a program for children up to three years old whose mothers were working. They would provide for an adequate number of licensed homes which would afford a family-type environment with no more than three or four children in each group. For children ages three to five they would provide two community houses, one rural and one in an urban poverty section, with classroom and playroom instruction, outdoor recreational facilities, with arrangements for a daily bath and hot meals. Qualified kindergarten instruction would be given to the five-year-olds, and nursery school instruction to the four-year-olds.

Gaston County advocated a preschool readiness program to operate six weeks before the opening of the school year. "Homemaking" instruction for mothers was planned as an additional aspect of the program.

All the other counties proposed creative variations of these illustrative proposals which would give preschool children a look at a fresher environment.

There were also proposals to give special attention to children in the primary grades. Caswell County proposed to employ a director of guidance and staff to help in organizing and carrying out a program of guidance for children with problems in the first four grades of school.

Durham County proposed a family unit action approach. The plan called for selecting six groups of about thirty families each, including children from four selected elementary schools. The first phase of the program would be to identify family needs and prepare a "Breakthrough Plan." Then the task force and supporting agencies would concentrate their efforts on solving the problems of the home while students would attend a special program through six grades. Experimental classes would include team teaching, remedial instruction, and counseling.

Lee County proposed for children beyond the third grade "the use of day camps, summer camps, and evening facilities where organized study and recreation on a year-round basis may be carried out."

Beaufort County suggested a vocational education program for both races, in response to the dropout rate, concentrating on the sixth and seventh grades. Bladen County came up with a program of vocational training, to begin at the sixth grade or earlier, for the prospective dropout, as indexed on their "dropout card."

There were many proposals for adult education. Alamance County, through its industrial education center, offered courses for illiterates in neighborhood areas selected as experimental sites. Cumberland County proposed the initiation of new programs to promote employer interest in providing training for illiterate employees.

Forsyth County proposed establishment of training programs to meet the needs of its unemployed; in some cases, basic reading and writing courses; in others, special training to prepare them for entry into the industrial education center. Franklin County suggested a year of on-the-job training for boys and girls sixteen to twenty-one who were out of school and unemployed.

Richmond-Scotland-Robeson Counties, "Tri-County Community Action," proposed a progressive program, in selected communities, of surveys, counseling, testing, vocational training in a wide range of courses, culminating in a job-placement program.

There were many school-related proposals, all designed to make education more meaningful and understandable. For example, Duplin, Wayne, and Greene Counties put forward the idea of establishing a youth motivation camp for underprivileged youth, thirteen to seventeen years old, to be held prior to the beginning of the school year, emphasizing nutrition, physical fitness, swimming, national heritage, religious atmosphere, educational motivation, and self-expression, and Nash and Edgecombe Counties proposed a "Student Volunteer Committee" to assist in teaching fundamental education.

There was special attention given to ways to stop dropouts. Cleveland County proposed a counseling service for potential dropouts, and a four-county mountain area, Cherokee, Clay, Graham, and Swain Counties, proposed classes for dropouts under twenty-five in literacy, academic, and vocational subjects, and college level classes. Orange and Chatham Counties proposed "A Pre-Dropout Project" to identify at the earliest the potential dropout, with an attempt to develop community and interagency coordination and skill in prompt preventive and therapeutic action.

Special attention was paid to economic conditions to help stabilize the family life of the children whose home circumstances were hampering their school possibilities. For instance, the Choanoke Area, consisting of five counties, wanted to set up a rehabilitation training program for displaced farmers, and Person County proposed a staff to implement the findings of the land-use study being conducted under the Area Redevelopment Act.

Macon County outlined an agricultural program for the future fresh marketing or processing of food crops.

Charlotte-Mecklenburg proposed using the regular school structure to operate several neighborhood centers for school readiness, health maintenance, and job opportunity, drawing in students and others from the neighborhood who might be helped by these special services.

Birth control was considered, with Harnett County suggesting classes in planned parenthood, child care, prenatal care, and home nursing. Pasquotank proposed a health project to identify, treat, and correct problems of indigent groups, with instruction for preschool children, students, and parents in health and hygiene.

Hundreds of other projects were outlined, and at first glance the list of efforts may appear to be a hodgepodge. Probably it is not. The hope of success for our North Carolina Fund experiments, and now the hope of success of the community action program of the Office of Economic Opportunity, is local drive, interest, innovation, direction, and motivation. No such national program could possibly see the daylight of success without the diversity and intensity of local leadership.

By mid-April, after the evaluation and visits to every community by the staff and Board teams, we selected the projects, ultimately eleven, which we hoped would be representative of the experiments we expected to carry forward.

To help in all these communities, the Fund organized the "North Carolina Volunteers," a program with a Peace Corps flavor. In the first year, the summer of 1964, we had one hundred college students. More than 750 applications, on short notice, were received from sixty college campuses.

These students were paid $22.50 a week and their keep. They worked in the preschool readiness projects, the boys' clubs, drove the bookmobile, served as welfare caseworker aides, all with zest and vitality. They not only invigorated the local community, but returned to the campus with a new feeling of relevance.

To help year-round in the communities, the Fund set up a program of recruiting and training young people sensitive to the difficulties of the people we sought to help. These are known as CATS, Community Action Technicians. They provide trained staff assistance, generate enthusiasm, and approach the problems as skilled technicians.

Mostly, however, success would depend on the involvement of volunteers. Had The North Carolina Fund done nothing but prompt local groups to take inventory, to include in their censuses for the first time "the invisible people," its efforts would have been crowned with success. For the first time, in many instances, the hazy, dimly seen figures who move about the shanties in a dreary pantomime suddenly were brought into clear focus as human beings whose mode of life made an ironic mockery of the Chamber of Commerce sign at the city limits: "A Good Place to Live and Work."

Our second guide described the reading-writing-arithmetic project—"The Comprehensive School Improvement Program," the Department of Public Instruction called it. This furnished information to the school superintendents, and advised them how they might enter the experiment covering preschool and the first three grades. For this we had $4 million, half of which was supplied by the Fund, from the Ford grant, and the other half supplied by state funds. This was to be used for the public school program in elementary education, unofficially called "The Three R's" or "The ABC Project." It was hammered out by Everett Miller, Epps Ready, John Ehle, and Clarence Faust.

In the third year it had some four hundred participating schools, and is ably directed by a former superintendent of the Gastonia schools, Woodrow Sugg. The simple object is to find ways that might be used in all the schools to make sure that by the end of the third grade all the children can read well, write acceptably, and figure correctly. The methods, approaches, and experiments would be many, but out of it all, we hoped, would come better ways of teaching beginners.

Here is how Charlotte *Observer* writer Hummerstone described one school's participation:

"There was a free readiness program at each school last summer, and those children are now in the project's special classes.

"There are three of these special first grade classes at each school, and each is treated as a single unit of ninety pupils. It is planned to have the same teachers stay with the same pupils through the next three years.

"To each three-teacher unit, a teacher aide has been assigned. She has at least two years of college, and her salary is paid from the funds set aside for the project. Her job is to help the teachers . . . by keeping records, maintaining discipline, giving slow learners special help, arranging field trips and rearranging furniture.

" 'It was what the teachers have asked for for years,' the principal said. 'Give me materials, give me time, give me someone to help with my records, and I'll teach. . . .'

"The project has also given each unit the resources to experiment with new concepts in teaching, such as:

"—Team teaching, where classes are combined for certain special lessons, with the teachers working together.

"—Ungraded classes, where pupils advance at their own rates, rather than an arbitrary grade-a-year pace.

"—Adding new subjects, such as modern math and science, at the first grade.

"Using newly-developed teaching equipment, such as flash cards, puzzles and educational toys, which are especially helpful in teaching the deprived child who is not familiar with books.

"The repercussions from the program are expected to be felt for years, but results have begun to appear already, the principal said. 'We are testing these kids intensively, and we can already see a difference. It's because of that additional six weeks last summer. That, and the new approach.'

"The teachers agree. 'The children who had pre-school training are scoring from ten to thirty points higher on tests than the others,' said Miss Inez Green, one of the teachers of the special classes. . . . Miss Green and her teacher's aide, Mrs. Harriet Frazier, are enthusiastically using their project money to buy long-needed teaching equipment, including record players and films, and to finance various field trips."

Miss Green and all the other teachers in the project are trying to overcome the defects, whatever they are, which cause so many third-graders to find they are behind in reading and writing and arithmetic. Because this program is experimental, many new methods, techniques, and arrangements will be tried.

The local superintendent proposes the program, shaping his own methods. The State Board, using the grant money, provides an adviser from one of our colleges and pays the costs of the innovations.

This has given us a chance to try out dozens of ideas. In addition to teachers' aides, team teaching, and ungraded classes, we have tried reducing the size of the first three grades to about half the average size, giving the good teacher fewer noses to wipe and more time to spend with each pupil. We have tried, in some places, the use of the "Initial Teaching Alphabet," which has done nobody any harm, and may prove a valuable teaching device.

Just as in the community action projects, the ABC Project utilizes local initiative. The fresh ideas springing from below will not give us uniformity, but we will have reached into more corners and we will have dug up more good answers.

This runs contrary to the "little bird" theory of government, which is an inherent pitfall and irresistible temptation for too many policy makers of government. These communities do not need to be fed by the mother bird who has already masticated the food. They can move out for themselves and come up with better ideas than we could have planned for them, if we give them a constant sense of freedom.

Local leaders in the community action projects need the ideas of the people living in poverty. They have learned that the beneficiaries of the projects are excellent consultants, and they have been brought in on advisory boards, and sometimes even on the governing boards, in every community project.

Now that the Office of Economic Opportunity has spread the community action programs from our eleven experimental projects across the breadth of the state, the chief danger of failure is that the guideline writers and policy formulators will forget the lesson that the strength and the best hope of success lie in community action, given freedom and flexibility to innovate and experiment and work within the limits of broad guidelines, but in their own best way with their peculiar requirements.

Out of the four hundred school experiments will come much general improvement of the schools, as well as improved techniques and organization of the first three grades. Out of the successful experiments will come new appropriations, from state and local taxes, to support the better ways. The probing before changing, using private funds and experimental public funds, not only has saved us money but has better illuminated the path we must follow in order to progress.

I don't know how we will be teaching second-graders ten years from now. I do know it will be done differently. I do know it will be done better than under any state plan we might have invented. I do know it will be better supported than if we had tried to get the money before demonstrating that there were better ways of teaching.

The seeds of this comprehensive improvement were our concern and desire for the Mellisas, the Honeys, and the little girls from Villa Heights. The North Carolina Fund was our expression of determination that education should reach all children, even if we had to fight through the ramparts of poverty in order to rescue, liberate, and teach them.

In describing our poverty program to the press, I said, "Some of this poverty is self-imposed and some of it is undeserved. All of it withers the spirit of children who neither imposed it, nor deserve it.

"These are the children of poverty who tomorrow will become the parents of poverty.

"We hope to break this cycle of poverty. That is what The North Carolina Fund is about.

"We will experiment, and seek to draw together the forces of organizations, government and education, to find the causes, and provide the new opportunities, and make North Carolina the place where the strong help the weak, and the weak grow strong."

The more we looked the more we found that should be done. So many, in so many places, had been too long neglected.

In addition to the multiple burdens of poverty, too many of our Negro students suffered a more specific handicap which hampered their success in the school system. In 1959 the median income of Negro families was less than half the median income of white families. Prosperity was not helping them much. The Negro median fell from 48 percent of the white median in 1949, to 43 percent in 1959. The dollar gap increased from $1,159 to $2,596.

Only 8 percent of Negro workers were in white-collar, clerical, or sales jobs compared to 37 percent of white workers. The unemployment rate among Negroes has been at least twice as high as the rate among whites since 1951. These statistics spell disadvantage, and disadvantage spells poor school performance.

When I visited the Negro schools on my regular school tours I was always impressed with their eagerness. They cleaned up, and painted gay signs, and presented special musical programs. The Boy Scouts wore their uniforms to direct our car to the proper stopping place.

I gave them the same message. "Stay in school. Take it seriously. Use your brain. This is the way to better jobs, to more income, to richer lives."

All this was pretty well received. But there was something hollow about it. "What," I thought, "if I were a Negro student, sitting there, listening, dreaming of what I might be. What would I think? Doesn't my daddy, I might be thinking, work as a porter at the airport? He told me to work hard, and he set a good example. He won a prize in high school for French and didn't he get his name in the paper not long ago when he had a conversation in French with some visiting farm experts from Tunisia? And what about Uncle Jake Withers? He was the valedictorian, and the banker gave him a medal which is on the wall at his home. And he's had steady work. He has a reputation for being very reliable. He drives one of the city trash trucks. Yes, Governor, my family knows the value of school. I'll promise to be like them."

I knew very well I wasn't telling the whole truth. True, without education there would be no hope. With education, their hopes at best would meet many frustrations.

To the handicap of poverty in many cases was added the handicap of color in all cases. I decided that since motivation was a basic ingredient of education, it fell to me to stimulate its development as much as I could. The appropriate motivation in this particular setting could come only from visible evidence that education would lead to jobs and a better life.

I thought about these children many times. Riding back from a speech one night I talked with Tom Lambeth, my administrative assistant. The next day I wrote out two statements and showed them to Graham Jones, my press secretary.

In January, 1963, I invited a group of people to breakfast, asked for their confidential advice, political and educational. They were convinced the course was right. Joel Fleishman checked the statements with many others, in and out of state government.

A few days after the breakfast I had a long-standing engagement to have lunch with a group of the North Carolina Press

Association meeting in Chapel Hill. Editors from all over the state would be there. It would be a good place, Graham thought, to announce a new program. Here, in part, is what I told them:

"The American Negro was freed from slavery one hundred years ago.

"In this century he has made much progress, educating his children, building churches, entering into the community and civic life of the nation.

"Now is the time not merely to look back to freedom, but forward to the fulfillment of its meaning. Despite great progress, the Negro's opportunity to obtain a good job has not been achieved in most places across the country.

"Reluctance to accept the Negro in employment is the greatest single block to his continued progress and to the full use of the human potential of the nation and its states.

"The time has come for American citizens to give up this reluctance, to quit unfair discrimination, and to give the Negro a full chance to earn a decent living for his family and to contribute to higher standards for himself and for all men."

I then announced "The Good Neighbor Program" by saying, "In North Carolina we will attempt to provide leadership for the kind of understanding America needs today."

I announced the creation of "The Good Neighbor Council," the chairman to be David S. Coltrane, a special consultant in my office, who had just retired as Director of the Department of Administration. He was perhaps the most experienced man in state government. As his vice-chairman I appointed retired Dean James T. Taylor of North Carolina College, a Negro. To them I assigned the tasks of (1) encouraging public and private employment of qualified people without regard to race and (2) urging all young people to become better trained and qualified for employment.

Calling on the mayors to establish similar local Good Neighbor Councils, I also called on private employers to participate, along with church leaders, pastors, and civic organizations. I announced that we were sending a memorandum to heads of state agencies directing them to formulate policies, if they had not already done so, that did not exclude qualified people from employment because of race.

As an assistant to Mr. Coltrane we placed on the state payroll an experienced and capable Negro woman, Mrs. Sara Herbin, who was instructed to seek qualified Negro applicants for jobs in state government. People such as Mrs. Herbin will play an increasingly important role in helping Negroes bridge their next big chasm: the space separating equal opportunity and the competitive labor market. For when the color of skin no longer is a job factor, skill and competence still will be.

This program had immediate favorable acceptance. It has worked well. In classifying things done, I think it is entirely appropriate to place the Good Neighbor Council under the general heading of "education."

Obviously this simple step would not remove the educational deficiencies long borne by the Negro. The inadequate education of the Negro is a cycle in itself, and we are just beginning to understand how to go about breaking it. But if we can open the jobs available in our society to those of ability without regard to race, then we can begin to fulfill the promise that education also leads to a better, fuller life for the Negro child.

The poor may always be with us, as some are so fond of saying. I do not doubt that they will. But the causes of poverty need not always be with an intelligent and advancing society. That is why we have been making special efforts to add to the educational advantages provided for the children of disadvantage.

CHAPTER X : The Catch-Up School

"I DIDN'T KNOW what is was to study," said the towhead. "I did, but I didn't want no part of it," replied the freckle-face.

This conversation between two students at North Carolina's Advancement School reveals in two sentences what many have called "the most exciting school in America."

The Advancement School is in Winston-Salem. It is housed in an old hospital. It is a residence school. At any one time it has only three hundred students. So what makes it exciting?

For one thing, it was planned in excitement. Its planning began late in the fall of 1963, and the doors opened in the fall of 1964. I proposed this target date to our original key group called to the Mansion to consider establishing a special residence school for what educators call "underachievers." They said the idea was good, that the school could be put together, but not likely on target. That would never do, I reminded them. My term of office would end in 1964. They promised to try to get the job done on time.

This was to be a new kind of school. U.S. Commissioner of

Education Francis Keppel, who knows how to encourage state initiative, and is ever anxious to promote a feasible idea, made us a planning grant of $80,000. In the Office of Education in Washington there can be found a report on Planning Grant No. F-033. It tells a story of excited educators who set about to plan "the most exciting school in America."

Everybody knows of bright students who get to junior high school dragging their feet. I'm not talking about the dull and the mentally limited. They are another group requiring special attention of another kind. I am talking about the average and the above average in intelligence who are just not getting much out of their schooling. They cannot or do not study efficiently. They have little interest in the academic side of school. They are listless in the classroom. They fall further and further behind and it appears that they will never catch fire and catch up. Why?

The truth is that no one really knows why. As one writer put it, "we're beginning to know our way around outer space but we know so little about the inner space of a child's mind; especially the part that tells him to get up and go, or lie down and quit."

The mystery of the age is not the moon. It is motivation.

We knew that we were on to something very complicated. We were struggling for the answers to motivating children who came from no common background. Their homes might be in slum sections or average neighborhoods. They include the so-called "advantaged underachievers" in the more wealthy suburban schools. Their parents might be professional or laboring people.

It was not a matter of native ability at all. It was something else. Perhaps they had a poor teacher at a critical time, or were in a bad school, or were in a troublesome neighborhood or part of a troubled family, or had parents who didn't encourage them. Maybe they were just slow starters. It might be that our methods of teaching simply do not reach a particular kind of child. For some reason, or, more likely, a variety of reasons, they just didn't pick up the ball and run.

We wanted to do something about it. John Ehle started

searching for the possibilities of what the Governor's office might do. He considered teaching devices, the exceptional teacher, the riddles of motivation. He talked to many people. He thought we needed to try some new ideas, to experiment, to change some concepts. He and I agreed that a residence school would probably provide us with the best laboratory.

John discovered a retired resident of Chapel Hill, Ralph Mc-Callister, former professor at the Maxwell School of Syracuse University and for seventeen years director of the Chautauqua Institute. We put him in charge of planning, and called to Raleigh scores of experts to help us design an experiment by which our schools might learn how to wake up the underachievers who were to be found in every single schoolroom across the state.

In October of 1963 we prepared "A Statement Concerning the North Carolina Advancement School." It was to serve the visiting and local consultants as guidelines of our hopes. It set forth the concept, leaving it to the consultants to evaluate the validity and develop the details:

"The North Carolina Advancement School, which the State is planning to start, is a residential school which will help annually 1400 junior and senior high school students of good potential. They will be helped to learn, in three-month terms, to read, write and do arithmetic better. It will use and evaluate modern teaching methods, seeking to help the State school system as well as these young people excel in performance, and it will be a center for teacher training.

"There will be no cost to the student for room, board or training.

". . . Students and teacher-trainees applying to the North Carolina Advancement School will be nominated by their Superintendents on a quota system determined by the School. . . . They must be eighth to twelfth grade students living in North Carolina, in good health, and they must be emotionally stable. A group of IQ and achievement tests and a physical examination will be given student nominees at the local school and the results sent to the Advancement School, along with a counselor's evaluation of the student's abilities and needs, and a request from the student himself, asking for admittance and indicating permission of his parents for him to attend. . . ."

We ultimately decided on eighth-graders to begin with, because we thought that this was the earliest age at which parents would want to let a child go away for an extended period of time, and because we felt that this was a crucial time in the educational process.

"Since this is also a teacher training school, it might be well to ask a superintendent to nominate seven students and one teacher as a group. These eight individuals might come from the same school, and thus have an association before they come to the Advancement School. . . .

"When the student arrives, he will be given a second group of tests. This second, more exhaustive testing period will be both diagnostic and motivational. . . . His instruction will be of three kinds, that which keeps him abreast of the work going on in his local school and class, that which helps him overcome his remedial problems, and that which helps him judge what he can become and achieve. . . .

"The instructional program will be oriented to the needs of the students and will place emphasis on the abilities of gifted teachers. At the same time, the fullest possible use of programed instruction will be made. The School might even experiment with the device of setting up a television receiver and a desk for each child, and a means by which he can answer questions on a station call-order system. If his answers are often wrong, he can easily be switched to another video tape recorder, one with the same material presented more slowly. . . . Other, more conventional forms of programed learning will be used, too. So will seminar-sized classes and individual coaching. . . .

"The master teachers, the counselors and the teacher-trainees will have time to work with small classes and to be with the students. Music, drama and other cultural activities will be carried on in an effort to involve the student in school activities, and in order to create at the School a general appreciation for human beings and human worth. . . ."

The preliminary statement continued:

". . . A suitable place for the School exists in Winston-Salem, in the city hospital, which will be vacated this coming spring. Three hundred fifty students and fifty teacher-trainees can be housed and taught there comfortably.

"The hospital is owned by the City of Winston-Salem. The Mayor, Mr. M. C. Benton, Jr., is prepared to ask the Board of Aldermen to make the hospital facilities available for the exclusive use of this School. . . .

"The administration of the School will fall to the State Board of Education. . . . This is not a local school in any sense; it will be the first school of its type in our country, and the School will be free to find people who have worked with these problems, who are aware of what new methods will achieve and what they won't achieve, and who can identify with the problems of these young people. The School will be free to find its personnel anywhere it chooses. . . ."

The counseling system at the school has been central to its purpose. The counselors live in the hall with the boys, tutor them in their deficiencies, brush away the homesick tears, and share their problems. Many of the counselors are returning Peace Corps volunteers, with experience in working with young people and an infectious enthusiasm for their jobs. As one newsman said when he was being shown through the school, "I've never seen a more gung-ho bunch of kids in my life."

"*Teacher Training.* This division of the School is to be limited to 50 teachers at a time, chosen from the same schools from which many of these students are to be taken. It is expected that they will be released by their local school system for a 12-week term. They will not be charged for room, board or tuition, and perhaps they will be paid something by their local school system. They will be asked to work as assistant teachers at the School, to help score tests, help the students with their work, help with the cultural and recreational programs. They will have courses prepared for them, and perhaps they will receive college credit for them from one of the existing institutions of the State. Many of the teachers will, on returning home, become local representatives of the School, helping the School select students, helping to start remedial courses and generally to improve the quality of instruction in their school, perhaps using materials prepared at the School. . . .

"These local teachers are one key to the success of the School's efforts to contribute to the school system as a whole. . . .

"*The Budget.* The State has money in sight or in hand to pay for about one-third of the cost of the School for the first three years of its operation. . . . The basic budgets are attached."

Mavis Kennedy, Washington journalist, has written an account of the planning and opening of the school, beginning with the first conference at the Governor's Mansion.

"Victorian elegance was the setting for mid-twentieth century conversation about education.

"To a youngster slumped in his seat in some North Carolina classroom, perhaps attentive, most probably not, a youngster who, each year, slipped a little further behind in school, and was now, perhaps, beginning to think of himself as 'one of the dumb ones,' it would have been inconceivable that the men and women in the Governor's Mansion were talking about him; making exciting plans for him; saying he was special and important and someone they wanted to know a lot better."

Miss Kennedy continued: "An initial 'Statement Concerning the North Carolina Advancement School' . . . was soon joined in the file . . . by proposals for grants, by lists of committees, by agenda for meetings, by reports on meetings, by budgets, by bills, by papers from interested experts, by inquiries from the press and from the public. . . ."

She picked out a flavor of the comments of the conferees at the first general planning session in February of 1964:

"Flexibility . . . we've got to be willing to start something with this youngster, and then be willing to stop and change if what we're doing doesn't seem right."

"The underachiever in reading usually has troubles in other areas. If we can help solve his reading problems, he'll improve in other areas, whether or not the Advancement School teaches them as specific subjects."

"Individual instruction may make the difference."

"Yes, but he mustn't become too dependent on teachers at the School, or he might not continue his progress at home."

"I wonder if the programed materials already available are going to suit his needs?"

"Well, if new materials have to be developed they should be usable in the public schools as well."

"You know, we may find that he's going to be influenced more by the cultural environment and by the physical surroundings than by what happens in the classroom."

"Don't want to make him discontented when he gets home. Can't have him contending with too great a divergence."

"He has to have a normal personality, or the School won't be able to help him. That is, we won't be attempting to work with youngsters with severe emotional problems."

"Volunteers . . . he has to be a volunteer and really like the idea of coming to the School, or we'll never get to first base with him."

"I like the idea of a visiting teacher from his school coming with him, as well as several other youngsters from the same school. The teachers can help take the edge off homesickness while he's at the School, and then help carry the program back home."

"Experimental or demonstration? Which will the Advance-

ment School be? Or will it be both? Yes . . . yes, it will *have* to
be both. We'll have to experiment in order to know what should
be demonstrated."

"Now one of the problems . . ."

". . . and special emphasis must be given . . ."

"A Learning Resources Center . . ."

". . . to evaluate the effectiveness . . ."

"The motivational patterns . . ."

"Afternoon meeting in the Governor's Mansion. Dinner there;
evening session, too. Next morning, final session in the Senate
Chamber of the Capitol. Soft North Carolina voices. Governor
Sanford and John Ehle and Ralph McCallister were aided in
representing the state by several others, including: Everett
Miller, Assistant State Superintendent of Public Instruction, and
Dr. I. E. Ready, Director of the Department of Community
Colleges. Perhaps the most soft-spoken of all, these two Southern
gentlemen quietly helped convey North Carolina's excitement
about education, and their own excitement about the Advance-
ment School.

"Active interest, working interest, contributive interest from
all echelons of North Carolina education is, as the out-of-states
could plainly see, at once a cause and an effect of an ever-
increasing focus on the schools as one of the most powerful
means of developing human resources. Rich and renowned Duke
University is as concerned with the loftiest reaches of research-
dom as any similarly favored institution, but there was Everett
Hopkins, Vice-President of Duke, helping plan what the Advancement School could do to reach the wellspring of motivation
within that youngster slumped at his desk, all unaware what a stir
he was causing. William C. Friday, President, and Donald Anderson, Vice-President of the University of North Carolina, met
with members of the Advancement School's general planning
committee. And so did Dallas Herring, Chairman of the North
Carolina Board of Education, and Charles Carroll, Superintendent
of Public Instruction for the State.

"Naming some, but not all of those who came from close by and from afar, is a limitation of space, not importance. Diverse in background, often in approaches and opinion as well, they shared a commitment to that youngster in the classroom. And that, ultimately, would make the idea work.

" 'The important thing about something like this is to do something,' says Dr. Howard Miller, Chairman of the Department of Psychology at North Carolina State University at Raleigh. 'If what you have isn't perfect in conception, theory, etc., okay; correct it later, but start!' "

We were going to need money. And we were going to need administrative and faculty leadership with verve and imagination.

The money would come from the Carnegie Corporation, a half million dollars, the first to show concrete faith in the concept of the Advancement School, a commitment made by President John Gardner even before we had obtained the planning grant from Francis Keppel. It would also come from the U.S. Office of Education, $1.4 million, with about the same from the state of North Carolina spread over a period of three years.

The leadership to give the school vitality appeared more difficult. Where could we find the best man in America to run this kind of new venture in education? Why, it wasn't difficult at all. The best man in America to run this kind of school was Gordon L. McAndrew, then heading the intercity project in Oakland, California, dedicated to the objective of upgrading the educational opportunities of 3,500 children from the slum areas. Doctor's degree from the University of California at Berkeley, experienced in positions of major responsibility in the Oakland public school system, brilliant, imaginative, concerned about children and education—he was our man.

The job of getting him was assigned to the superintendent of schools of Scarsdale, New York. And this wasn't such an illogical choice, because Harold Howe had already signed on with North Carolina to head the brand-new Learning Institute of North Carolina. LINC would have the responsibility of directing the

Advancement School for the State Board of Education. Mc-
Andrew talked to Howe, he visited North Carolina, he knew he
had only a few months to put together a staff, he saw that the
buildings were not ready, he understood that the federal grant
had not been approved.

The audacity of the proposition captivated him.

"When I got back home I still just couldn't see it," remembers
Dr. McAndrew. "The whole thing seemed impossible. And yet, I
couldn't get it out of my mind. If we could bring it off, it would
be the most exciting thing in education in the United States."

And so the man from the gold rush country packed up his wife
and two children and headed east for explorations in the Sea-
board State where the first English settlers had explored almost
four hundred years earlier. He opened his school on schedule
with a remarkable faculty gathered from the reaches of the
nation.

Is it working? Are its students catching up? Are the lessons of
any value to the thousands in the public schools who, for lack of
space, can never attend the Advancement School? We are beginning to see the form of the answer. It will work.

Tommy Smith had come to the Advancement School from a
small eight-grade school in North Wilkesboro. He was never
sullen but his teachers were troubled over his inability to rise to
his potential. He was a member of the first class that attended the
school.

One morning, six months after the boy left to return home, Dr.
McAndrew got a call from the principal in the school asking him
to give the commencement address on graduation night. The
busy director of the North Carolina Advancement School could
hardly have been expected to take time to make a speech to a
small rural eighth-grade class graduating to high school. That is,
not until the principal explained why he was inviting Dr. Mc-
Andrew: Tommy Smith had just been named valedictorian of his
graduating class.

Ralph McCallister, in discussing the school with the superintendents of schools from across the state, quoted Dr. J. R. Zacharias "that investment in research to create new models of instruction can multiply the effectiveness with which education funds are spent, and the task of educational research and development is to learn how to provide for all students the education an exceptional teacher provides for a few."

"The Advancement School," said McCallister, "had its origin in this atmosphere of concern shared by all of you to improve education for our children, to make more effective use of the funds available for education, and to find answers to some of the questions plaguing our schools.

"It was proposed that the school be designed to diagnose educational problems and seek to deal with them. It would search for and design new materials and methods, test them out to the end of creating new models of instruction so that the effectiveness with which educational funds are spent might be multiplied.

"This, it was said by a North Carolina Superintendent of Schools, is just what he would like to do in his own school if he had the staff, the funds and the flexibility to undertake such a program. The North Carolina Advancement School represents, in effect, a pooling of problems, of interests and resources to help improve the education of all the children."

The returns have not been counted, and the election is not yet completed. It appears that the campaign is being won.

The parents, the principals, and the students who have gone back home believe, with wholeheartedness, that the school is a marvelous answer to the prayers of many parents.

There are some instances of near-miraculous results. One boy came to the Advancement School with his thumb in his mouth, and his eyes turned downward as if a gaping manhole was always waiting to swallow him up. One day he knocked on Dr. McAndrew's door and asked if he could speak with him a minute.

Shyly, he asked if he could sit at the switchboard and take the incoming phone calls and the messages for the school the next day. The boys take turns sitting at the front desk acting as the answering service for the school, and get to use a loudspeaker to summon counselors, and teachers, and other boys to the phone. It's a big honor, but it can get frantic at times. Dr. McAndrew looked at this boy who had been such a misfit and asked,

"How do I know you can do the job?"

And with that the boy launched into a monologue pretending he had a phone in his hand and that calls were coming in and punctuated it all with imitations of the buzzer, the loudspeaker, and the ringing phone. "North Carolina Advancement School . . . Dr. McAndrew? . . . One moment . . . Don't go away, I'll put you on hold . . . I'm sorry Dr. McAndrew isn't in . . . Can I take a message? . . . Yes, I'll see that he gets it . . . Thank you so much . . . Bye."

When he had finished he looked up for a reaction from a startled director.

"You've got yourself a job."

Later, Dr. McAndrew found out that the boy had been hanging around the answering desk for days; and that the previous night his counselor had heard this strange talk coming through the door of his room and had gone in to see if anything was wrong.

"No. Nothing's wrong. I've got an important interview in the morning."

When this boy left the Advancement School thirty days later he was a different person. He stood tall and looked at you and there was no more thumbsucking. The state of North Carolina had altered his life.

And will the ripples go out to all the girls and boys who are now slumping at their desks, loafing through school life? We think so. We hope so. As Dr. Miller said, the most important thing was to start.

CHAPTER XI : Learning About Learning

"WE ARE NOT going to finish the job of improving education in four years." I sounded this warning at every appropriate opportunity. I hoped we would not make a massive spurt upward and then settle back into relaxed or indifferent resignation that we had done our best.

It was and must always be our purpose to develop a system of schools which neglects no child and disregards no talent. If the old ways didn't work, then we must try new ways. If the new ways didn't work, or weren't fully effective, we couldn't give up. We had to try again, or redesign, or go another way, for we could not waste the resources of the state. Our daily ambition was to shape a school with universal goals, but as the four years were ending I realized more than ever that we had just begun. The more you do to improve education the more you discover what is yet to be done. Each breakthrough opens a window on another unexplored frontier.

The people of North Carolina had demonstrated their willingness to support new taxes and to applaud new appropriations for the advancement of education. They had borne out the contention that, in their desire to enrich the schools for their children, they were ahead of timid public officials. They have also demonstrated that a state government can effect more forceful leadership, for more general improvement, than can any other level of governmental authority. Local government can and must provide initiative, interest, and substantial financial and moral support. Many have set exceptional examples in education, but their results are limited in reach. It takes the state to prompt action to find *every* child and touch every talent.

It is not enough to have the finest school system in the country if the adjoining district has one of the worst. Ultimately the product of the weak district will dilute the prosperity of the more fortunate products of the excellent system. Correcting this kind of damaging inequity requires state action.

The federal government can improve its contributions to education. It can nourish research and provide additional money for the general support of schools. It can also stymie school improvement, as can the states, if the policy makers do not leave to local leaders sufficient freedom for improvement. The able U.S. Commissioner of Education suggests that the federal government is a "junior partner" in the business of education. That is good, but the states have the capacity to do far more than they have done, and they must start moving more rapidly if they intend to remain the senior partners.

All the steps forward in the quest for better educational opportunities have not been recounted in this story of North Carolina action. The steps by the state have been stretched even wider by the commitment expressed in the board rooms of county commissioners, in the schoolhouses, in almost every classroom, and in the institutions of learning across the state. There are many other concrete examples.

For example, there is the Southern School Improvement Center at Duke University, designed to put sparkle into dull-eyed youngsters from ages two through eight who had the misfortune to be born into poor families. Supported by the Ford Foundation, this extensive experiment is an outgrowth, I believe it is fair to say, of The North Carolina Fund Durham project, "Operation Breakthrough."

There was the experimental program in vocational and technical orientation courses in the junior high schools, originated by the 1963 state appropriation of $1.5 million. The state department and local boards are opening for many youngsters vocational vistas far beyond the agriculture and woodworking skills into which too many training programs had been cramped.

There was the Stay-in-School statewide project of the Optimists Clubs.

There were the Belmont Players in Gaston County, the Shakespeare productions by Lyn Ely's Theatre-In-Education, and a general renaissance in the arts.

There was the $100 million state bond issue passed by a public vote on November 3, 1964, to aid local governments in the construction of school buildings.

There were the increased expenditures from local governments of supplements to the operational support of the schools, from $43 million in 1961–62 to $56 million in 1963–64.

There is the continuing support under Governor Dan K. Moore, with $71,266,651 in state secondary enrichment funds appropriated in 1965, pushing the biennial total to $604,693,784, as compared with $350,118,708 for 1959–61. The total state funds for all education had been increased from the 1959–61 total about $400 million to $748 million in the 1965–67 budget. The state has assumed a role of approximately 80 percent in the support of the public schools.

There are hundreds of other examples. Interest and action begot interest and action. North Carolina had set out to grapple for educational leadership by asking itself "But what about the people?"

John Gardner has written an invigorating book, *Self-Renewal*, in which he ably expresses the necessity for society, for institutions, and for individuals to engage in never-ending efforts to refresh and renew their attitudes, their purposes, their standards, their commitments, their ethical values, and their moral views.

"If society hopes to achieve renewal, it will have to be a hospitable environment for creative men and women. It will also have to produce men and women with the capacity for self-renewal . . . [who] need not fall into a stupor of mind and spirit. . . . They need not relinquish . . . the resilience of youth and the capacity to learn and grow."

There is indeed no end to the process of improving and maturing, and this applies to society and to the individual, and to the institutions of the individual and society. It is particularly true of the schools, for if the schools become immune to change and unreceptive to fresh ideas, the means of self-renewal are lessened, perhaps fatally.

"Education," Mr. Gardner reminds us, "can lay a broad and firm base for a lifetime of learning and growth. The individual who begins with such a broad base will always have some capacity to function as a generalist, no matter how deeply he chooses to specialize. Education at its best will develop the individual's inner resources to the point where he can learn (and will *want* to learn) on his own. It will equip him to cope with unforeseen challenges and to survive as a versatile individual in an unpredictable world. Individuals so educated will keep the society itself flexible, adaptive and innovative."

If education has this significant role in self-renewal, it must within itself be self-renewing. We wanted to see the means of self-renewal built into the North Carolina system of education. To assure further criticism, to have it so that we would always be taking an open look at new needs and old failures, we needed to invoke the broadest possible support. Also it was completely true that research had too long been neglected in education generally.

There were so many things about education that we did not know and were not learning. I reminded a group of businessmen assembled in Atlantic City in 1963 that we had not supported for education the kind of research without which their own businesses would not have flourished.

"There are ways," I suggested to them, "to accelerate learning, procedures of teaching barely explored, processes of acquiring and retaining knowledge more profound than we have ever realized were possible." It was imperative that we institute such research.

Neither did we have a clearinghouse for ideas to serve as a source of original research and as a conduit for the transmission of ideas advanced and developed elsewhere. For example, the accumulated knowledge about how to educate the talented outran our ability to collect and correlate it. Exciting improvements and discoveries were occurring around the nation, and in other parts of the world, but we had no agency collecting, digesting, and relaying them to our schoolrooms. If a teacher had a brilliant and workable idea, or tried something different and good, in all likelihood the innovations traveled no farther than the sound of his voice. We lacked the conduit.

If teachers and administrators saw needs and wanted answers, they had no ready place to go to request experimentation.

If a university devised something demonstrably useful in teaching, there remained a job of selling which it was not necessarily equipped to do. It also labored under a degree of suspicion that "these ivory tower people didn't know, really, what the schoolteachers need to know." Furthermore, it was awkward for public or private university people in research to get the desirable connecting link with the colleges heavily involved in teacher training.

In the early part of 1964 I was in Durham for a meeting of The North Carolina Fund. I asked the President of the University of North Carolina, William C. Friday, and Duke University's president, Douglas Knight, to have breakfast with me. I invited, also, Dr. Carroll, who could not come, but Dallas Herring, Chairman of the State Board of Education, there for the Fund meeting, was able to attend. I also invited Mrs. Mary Biddle Semans of the Duke Endowment and Duke University Trustees. I wanted her ideas which had been very helpful in other projects, and also I thought she might have to assure Dr. Knight that they could get up the money I was going to ask Duke to contribute.

"I'd like for us to explore," I told them, "an evaluation and research center, drawing into partnership everybody in North Carolina concerned with education. In the colleges the participation should be interdisciplinarian and should extend beyond the schools of education, thus drawing in the new strength of other departments. It should combine all the forces of the public and private universities, all of their departments, all colleges, the public schoolteachers and school administrators, and the state administration. We should include every source capable of contributing something to improved schools, and every position capable of putting new approaches to practical use."

They agreed it should be done. John Ehle would work with them to develop the structure and the arrangements.

Dr. Carroll, I have always appreciated, did not take a protective attitude. He welcomed frank opinions and constructive fault finding. I told him about the breakfast he had missed and he said, "Fine, let's do it."

Dr. William C. Archie, Director of the Board of Higher Education, enthusiastically joined in for the colleges.

John Ehle talked to many people, and one day came in and said let's call it "Link."

"Where in the world did you get that name?" I asked him.

"The initials of the Learning Institute of North Carolina—you spell it LINC."

So we took the name and we incorporated a private nonprofit corporation, dedicated to bringing together "in cooperative action educators from the various strata of education in our State, public, private and governmental," with authority to make contracts with public or private institutions, to operate schools, programs, and other projects, to operate as a planning agency to explore educational potentials, to design and operate research and exploratory programs and schools in cooperation with other institutions, to make grants to individuals whether public or private in support of its purposes, to conduct basic and applied research studies, to develop curricular materials, and to disseminate information, all "in its search for ways to improve learning."

This set of prerogatives could have made the educators nervous, except that it was their organization. The charter members contributing $60,000 each to the annual administrative budget were Duke University, the State Board of Education, the University of North Carolina, and The North Carolina Fund. We had no trouble finding the money to get it started.

For almost four years we had two policies about state money. First, we insisted that appropriated money not be spent if the needs were not clear, and we set a new record in returning funds to the state treasury. Second, we were always willing to transfer funds, when possible, to try out something new and promising. This involved an infinitesimal part of the budget, but it promoted a lively flow of fresh ideas. We used this technique to set up LINC.

The Board of Directors would be: the State Superintendent of Public Instruction, the President of Duke University, the President of the University of North Carolina, the Chairman of the State Board of Education, the Director of the North Carolina Board of Higher Education, the Chairman of The North Carolina Fund, and one teacher, one principal, and one superintendent.

In addition the State Board of Education would designate two other members and one each would be designated by Duke, the University of North Carolina, the Board of Higher Education, and The North Carolina Fund. The Fund, incidentally, designated

Governor Dan K. Moore, who subsequently was elected president of LINC in my place.

Our hope was to gain wide acceptance by wide representation, and to assure the full use of all developments by wide participation.

To head this broad-based and ambitious agency, the Board, on the nomination of Dr. Carroll, elected a distinguished and experienced educator, Harold Howe, II, then superintendent of the schools of Scarsdale, New York.

It is his job to keep everybody working together in North Carolina's "search for ways to improve learning." He came to the job in the summer of 1964, and speaking to the assembled school superintendents, told them "the things I have said this evening constitute brave hopes rather than any report of specific involvement. In a new organization, this is a necessity. Over the next year or two, with your help and with all the energy and imagination we can muster in what will be a slowly growing staff of carefully selected and competent people, this new organizaton will hope to become both accepted and useful."

LINC will be involved in many endeavors, and will be as useful as the educators care to make it by their own acceptance and participation. One of its first projects was to work with the University Department of Psychology to develop, in cooperation with other departments and the local school board, an experimental project, the Day Care Center and Laboratory at the Frank Porter Graham School in Chapel Hill.

The early purposes and hopes are described in a statement publicized by the LINC directors. It is to be "a state-wide cooperative effort. Its tools include its own staff and the research resources of the universities, colleges and schools of the State. Its principal laboratory is the North Carolina public school system. And its directors and staff seek the best minds in education in the State and country to assist in its programs. . . .

"In performing this function, the Learning Institute serves, as its abbreviated name suggests, as the 'link' between educational research and development and the application of promising findings in the schools of North Carolina."

The State Board of Education assigned to LINC the operational responsibility for the Advancement School, since the operation of schools is not a function of a state policy board. The details were arranged, a contract was signed, and the money we had obtained from the U.S. Commissioner of Education and the Carnegie Corporation for the operation of the school would be channeled through LINC. This was to be an important laboratory of learning.

As I reflect on the manner in which I have related this story of North Carolina's efforts to improve education I have the feeling I have made it appear that every time we came upon a good idea, everybody eagerly joined to put it into operation. Such was not the case, and those who would work to improve any governmental function must enter the battle prepared to fight.

For example, LINC and the Advancement School were almost killed at birth. Every step of the establishment of the relationship between LINC, the State Board of Education, and the Advancement School was approved by the Attorney General. But the Auditor objected. He did not agree that there was legal authority for state agencies to contract with LINC. He threatened complete disapproval. Thus the investment of more than a year of planning was jeopardized.

I wanted to blast away. Of course, without question, the Board of Education had a right to contract with LINC. We had acted in good faith, prudently, and with approval of every step by the Attorney General, himself an elected official and no appointee of mine. I was sure we would win a public debate on this issue.

In the closing days of my administration there wasn't time for debate. For a tense week we negotiated. We could have dismissed his objections, but time was short, and to engage in a hurried and indecisive public debate would have clouded public confidence in LINC.

The Auditor finally recanted, somewhat. He could work it out to his personal satisfaction, he thought, if the staff members of the Advancement School were made employees of the State Board of Education. This technicality was without any substance, but it would violate the terms of the federal and Carnegie grants.

So, by telephone and letter we asked the U.S. Commissioner of Education and Carnegie to amend their grants and allow this arrangement. They did, by return mail, and the Advancement School sailed on and the Learning Institute sidestepped a mortal blow.

There will always be those who fear change. They are mostly good and conscientious people, but in governmental affairs they have failed to understand that we build the state and the nation by investing in human capital. Without dreaming they were doing harm, their "hold-the-line" attitudes have greatly retarded the progress of North Carolina.

In the process of negotiating the LINC arrangements I had a long conference with a Council of State member whose help I needed in mollifying the Auditor. He agreed to help.

As he left he said to me, in a helpful tone, "You know the trouble with your budget office is that they should be trying to keep agencies from spending money. Instead they are always helping them find ways to spend it."

As he closed the door I realized he had inadvertently paid me the finest compliment I was likely to receive. We had indeed tried to help all our agencies become the creative servants of our citizens, better accomplishing their missions of affording broader opportunities for all people. We had not considered state government a caretaker of things as they were, but an innovator of what we might become.

We had tried to heed Carl Sandburg's poetry, always measuring our decisions by asking, "What about the people?" He called them the "reservoir of the human reserves that shape history."

But people do not act alone. They have joined together in

government for action and expression that shapes whatever their history is to be. The instrument of their imprint on the sands of memory is responsive government—a lantern of innovation and progress, bold in the discharge of its mission, equal to the dreams of its citizens, and reflective of the best that is in them.

If this nation dare promise greatness, then education is the buttress of the covenant. Self-government is not a detached and supervisory force. It is people. All that government can do for education will be repaid in self-sustenance, as it helps what is really itself to reach for the horizons and beyond. It is through education that government lifts to a more civilized state the people it serves, and serves in a more civilized way the idea that gave it life.

Index

DATE DUE

DEMCO 38-297